Backyard Roughing It Easy

DIAN THOMAS

Backyard Roughing It Easy

Unique recipes for outdoor cooking, plus great ideas for creative family fun—all just steps from your back door

THE DIAN THOMAS COMPANY
SALT LAKE CITY, UTAH

Distributed by Betterway Books, an imprint of F&W Publications, Inc., 1507 Dana Avenue, Cincinnati, OH 45207. (800) 289-0963

01 00 99 98 97   5 4 3 2 1

Library of Congress Cataloging-in-Publication Data

Thomas, Dian
    Backyard Roughing It Easy: unique recipes for outdoor cooking, plus great ideas for creative family fun, all just steps from your back door / Dian Thomas.
        p. cm.
    Includes index.
    ISBN 0-9621257-5-X (pbk. : alk. paper)
    1. Outdoor cookery.   2. Camping.   I. Title.
TX623.T46   1997
641.5'78--dc21   97-965
                                                                          CIP

NOTICE: The information in this book is true and complete to the best of our knowledge. All recommendations are made without guarantees on the part of the author/publisher. The author/publisher disclaims all liability in connection with the use of this information.

Editors
    Dianne King
    Dondrea Warner
    Fiona Willis

Illustrators
    DeeAnn Thaxton
    Cathleen Carbery-Shaw

Photographer
    Brian Twede

Production Coordinator
    Kimberly Chamberlain

Recipe Development
    Guida Ponte
    Pika Nielson

Cover & Interior Designer
    Sandy Kent

Layout
    Cathleen Carbery-Shaw

Acknowledgments

Special thanks to my parents, Julian and Norene Thomas, who first introduced me to the fun that can be had in your own backyard. Bill Brohaugh had the vision and encouraged me to prepare this volume. A very special thanks to Fiona Willis, Dianne King, and Dondrea Warner who worked with me to sculpture my words and bring special meaning to my ideas. Kim Chamberlain's tireless support and organization kept us all on track during the development of this book. Professional chef and friend, Guida Ponte worked with me to develop many of the recipes—sharing with me the flair of the food from her homeland, Portugal. Pika Nielson used her unique talents to polish and edit the recipes. Using his creative eye, Brian Twede captured the photographs that enhance the words in this book. Many thanks to DeeAnn Thaxton, whose artistic ability never ceases to amaze me. Thank you, Sandy Kent, for designing the cover of the book, which reflects the essence of backyard fun, and Cathleen Carbery-Shaw for using your creativity to make the pages of this book come to life.

Table of Contents

About the Author

Dian Thomas: genuine, uncomplicated ingenuity. TV personality and best-selling author, Dian has used her creativity to teach and entertain audiences for more than 20 years. Her clever ideas for cooking, crafts, entertaining and outdoor life have been shared with millions. As a regular family member of ABC's *Home* show for six years and NBC's *Today* show for eight years, she has become known as an advocate of fun, innovative creations and tips for easy living. Dian's philosophy is HAVE FUN! Her best-selling books *Roughing It Easy, Fun at Home with Dian Thomas* and *Today's Tips for Easy Living* have made her a much-sought-after demonstrator, and she travels extensively doing national and local television shows throughout the country. Dian holds a master's degree in home economics and has served as a consultant to several Fortune 500 companies.

Dedication

Dedicated to my nieces and nephews: Julie, Tiffany, Tamara, Michael, Matthew, Camilla, Mary, Jared, Sarah, Derek, Robyn, Emily, Rachel, Cameron, Daniel, and Rebekah.

Thank you for all the memories we have created in my backyard.

Foreword

A home is the heart of the family, but we shouldn't be limited by four walls when we are building our home environment. Some of the best memories I have of my childhood were created just outside the confines of our home, in our backyard. My brothers and I turned our yard into a paradise with some planning, a little work and a lot of fun. One summer we spent weeks designing and constructing ourselves a swimming pool using scrap pipe left at a nearby work camp, canvas, and wax colored with blue crayons to waterproof the pool. It didn't matter that the pool itself only lasted a few weeks after one of us got carried away playing Tarzan. Most of the fun we had came as we worked together to build it. But the real treasure is the memories of playing and working together that will last a lifetime.

I remember spending hours in our backyard with my family. We built tree houses and decorated the interiors. One spring we built a pen for a new baby lamb and spent months bottle feeding it. I even remember saving every penny I could get my hands on to buy a croquet set, just to have another reason to head outside with my family.

To this day, the backyard is still a major gathering place for my family—probably for many of you as well. But don't limit your fun to sitting on the patio after dinner. With a little planning, you can turn your backyard into an important element in bringing your family together. I hope this book can be a guide to bringing you as much backyard fun as I have always had.

Introduction

Every year hundreds of thousands of people head to America's national parks or its other wilderness areas trying to reclaim the calm and freedom that comes with venturing into the great outdoors. But in today's world where time has become so precious, you may be happy to find out you don't have to load up the family and head for the hills when you get the urge to commune with Mother Nature. In fact, you only need to look as far as your backyard or patio for a rewarding outdoor experience.

If you're looking for the pleasures of sleeping under starry skies, eating food cooked over glowing coals, and being outdoors with your family, why not camp out at home? It offers a refreshing activity for families with young children who would like to go camping, for parents who can't get time off from work for a long vacation, and even for grandparents whose grandchildren visit during the summer. A backyard campout is also a great time to teach outdoor skills to would-be campers and to test new camping equipment and techniques. And don't forget some of the more traditional outdoor family activities too: bike riding together, visiting a nearby park, fishing, hosting an outdoor slumber party, enjoying a cookout at the beach, planting a garden or any variety of other ideas.

But if you're thinking you don't have the equipment to throw any sort of outdoor activity, never fear. This book will show you how to take ordinary household items such as the ironing board, wheelbarrow, and flowerpots and turn them into innovative and fun outdoor accessories for your next party or barbecue. It has tips on the best kinds of grills to use, and how to keep the fires burning. It has details on how to cook using spits, sticks and grills, and it even gives you some tried-and-true recipes you can use at your next outdoor fiesta. This book will also show you some fun and easy ways you can serve your next meal outside.

So get ready for an adventure right outside your back door, and you'll fulfill your need for outdoor fun and—you could even spark your creativity, too.

CHAPTER 1

GRILLS AND SUCH

There are a variety of commercial grills available for the would-be outdoor chef, and that's what most people turn to when they are ready to do some outdoor dining. There are many different grills to choose from, probably the most popular being the gas grill. But don't let that make your decision for you; with a little bit of reading you should be able to find the grill which will precisely suit your needs. And if you're on a tight budget, don't worry. We'll also show you how you can improvise with some common household items and create your own grill.

Hibachi

A hibachi is a small charcoal grill, and its size is its biggest advantage. Because it's so small, the hibachi will allow you to grill on your patio, at the beach or in the woods. Most hibachis are made of cast iron. They come in various sizes so you can determine just how much room you'll need to do the kind of cooking you plan. But keep in mind that because of the hibachi's small size, meals will be limited to a few people.

Figure 1-1. Hibachi

Open Brazier

The open brazier is a very popular type of commercial cooker consisting of a grill suspended over a shallow bowl for coals. It can be found in several sizes, is usually lightweight, and has wheels on the legs for easy moving. You'll want to look for one that allows you to move the grill up and down to regulate the heat. You'll find it is excellent for cooking flat pieces of meat such as hamburgers, fish, chicken and steaks.

Figure 1-2. Open brazier

Kettle Grill

This grill allows the chef to barbecue larger pieces of food than other charcoal grills; in fact, the lid allows it to function much like an oven. Dampers on the top and bottom of a kettle grill can be opened to raise the temperature of the grill or closed to lower it. Cooking with the lid on gives a more uniform temperature and cooks food much like a Dutch oven would.

Figure 1-3. Kettle grill

Gas Grill

Gas grills are quickly gaining popularity because of their convenience. The gas grill eliminates the need to build a fire and the need to wait for the coals to heat up before you cook anything. That means you can start barbecuing just minutes after you turn it on. Gas grills have the advantage of easily controllable, consistent heat which makes cooking easier. And because they don't use charcoal, there

Figure 1-4. Gas grill

isn't any mess to clean up. The most common units use bottled gas; others use natural gas. While most gas grills are large patio units, there are portable units available as well. A gas grill generally costs more than other units, but if it is used frequently, the cost will even out.

Improvised Grills

If you don't want to buy a commercial grill but do want to do some barbecuing at your next outdoor party, you can make your own grill. A good backyard grill can be made from a child's wagon or even a garbage can lid. Here are some really fun ideas for a unique cooking adventure.

Figure 1-5. Wheelbarrow with dirt, foil and briquets

Wheelbarrow Grill

The metal wheelbarrow you have parked in the garage can make a versatile barbecue that will handle a whole meal. You will also need a few bricks, some foil and dirt. The great advantage of this grill is that you can wheel it wherever you want and it's just the right height to roast marshmallows or hot dogs from a lawn chair. The wheelbarrow also provides enough space for a rotisserie and a grill, as well as for direct cooking on the coals.

First, fill the wheelbarrow with about six inches of gravel, sand or dirt, just enough to insulate it from the heat. For efficient cooking with charcoal briquets, cover the area where the briquets will be placed with extra-heavy-duty aluminum foil. The foil will keep the coals from sinking into the dirt, and it insures that air will circulate to keep the briquets burning. Stack the briquets in the center of the wheelbarrow and light them. When they're hot, spread them over the foil. And finally, slide a pair of oven mitts over the handles of the wheelbarrow so they will be handy while you are grilling.

Once the briquets are burning, line the sides of the wheelbarrow with bricks, then place a large grilling rack across them for barbecuing flat pieces of meat. (For easy cleaning on any grill, spray the rack with nonstick cooking spray before using it.) You can regulate the cooking temperature by taking away bricks to raise the heat and adding them to decrease it. The most efficient grill height is about four to six inches above the coals. If you simply want to use the coals for stick cooking, don't bother about the bricks or the rack.

If you're a little more adventurous, you may want to try some other arrangements:

- **Rotisserie, grill and open coals**—use bricks on the back for a rotisserie, bricks just in front to support a wire rack, and then leave an open space for cooking over open coals.
- **Rotisserie and grill**—stack bricks at the back for a rotisserie and bricks along the side with a rack on them for a grill.
- **Grill**—place bricks on the four corners of the wheelbarrow and place a grilling rack on them.
- **Open coals**—cook directly on or over coals using foil or stick cooking methods.

Figure 1-6. Wheelbarrow grill set up for rotisserie, grill and open coal cooking

- **Cooking on hot bricks**—lay bricks side by side right on the dirt (do not put foil over the dirt) and start the fire on bricks. Then push the fire to one side to cook directly on the bricks. This type of cooking works well whether you use a hardwood fire or charcoal briquets—just make sure to call your local fire department to find out whether you are allowed to have a wood fire in your backyard. Brick bisquits are delicious cooked on hot bricks.

Figure 1-7. Wood fire in a wheelbarrow

Figure 1-8. Brick bisquits cooking on hot bricks

There are a couple of things you should keep in mind when improvising your own grill: Do not use refrigerator racks as grills. Some contain a harmful substance that is released when the racks are heated. Also, if you intend to reuse the grill, cover the wheelbarrow after the briquets are out so the dirt doesn't get wet. Moisture will tend to rust out the bottom of your wheelbarrow. If you keep it covered, a load of dirt will last the whole summer.

Child's Wagon Grill
Fill the wagon with dirt and follow basic directions given for the wheelbarrow grill.

Figure 1-9.
Child's wagon grill

Metal Garbage Can Lid Grill

Another type of improvised grill can be made from a metal garbage can lid or almost any metal container that can hold dirt for insulation. Turn the lid over to rest on three bricks, and then fill it with dirt. Cover the dirt with extra-heavy-duty foil and place briquets in a pile. Then light the briquets, place bricks along the sides and place a grill on top of the bricks.

Figure 1-10. Garbage can lid grill

Tin Can Grill

Here's an inexpensive and easy way to make a grill that is portable and is terrific if you don't have a lot of space. All you need is a large coffee can, metal cutters and a pair of safety gloves. First, starting at the open end of the can, cut 2-inch-wide parallel slits down the sides of the can. Cut down to about 3 inches from the bottom. Then bend the strips away from the center of the can, flaring them out to make a low basket-like container. Next, fill the bottom of the can with dirt and cover the dirt and strips with aluminum foil. You now have a shallow bowl-shaped grill. Place the charcoal on top of the foil and lay the grilling rack on top of the metal strips. It is important that the distance from the grilling rack to the charcoal is at least 3 to 4 inches—you may have to adjust the angle of the strips to achieve this distance. In just minutes you will have created a small grill that gives big results.

Figure 1-11. #10 can

Figure 1-12. #10 can cut and filled with dirt

Figure 1-13. #10 can covered in foil and filled with briquets

Figure 1-14. Tin can grill

Bricks and Cinder Blocks

You can also cook a delicious outdoor meal simply by building a barbecue using bricks or cinder blocks, a grilling rack, charcoal briquets and aluminum foil. Place foil on the ground and put bricks on the foil to support the rack used for grilling the meat. Arrange briquets on the foil and light them. Use a cookie cooling rack or an oven rack to cook on. To achieve the perfect cooking temperature for the type of food you are preparing, you may have to experiment with the number of bricks you use. The cinder block setup is made the same way.

Figure 1-15. Brick grill

Figure 1-16. Cinder block grill

Backpacker Rack

This is an easy grill to set up on an open dirt area in the backyard. Backpacker racks can usually be bought at a sporting goods store. Coals are placed on the ground and the rack sits on its legs about 6 to 8 inches above them. If the dirt is loose or sandy, place a piece of heavy-duty aluminum foil over it to keep the briquets from settling into the sand or dirt, which would cause the heat to be cut off.

The backpacker rack is ideal for regulating heat. To increase the intensity of the heat, simply push the rack into the ground. To lower the heat, pull the rack up.

Figure 1-17. Backpacker rack

Flowerpot Grill

If you don't have a lot of room to grill or just want to cook up something on the balcony, a clay flowerpot grill is the way to go, and it's easily stored, too. Use a nonglazed clay pot at least 11 inches high and 11 inches in diameter. Fill it with dirt or gravel to within 4 to 5 inches of the top. Then bank the dirt up on the sides of the flowerpot so the charcoal will not come into direct contact with it. Cover the dirt or gravel with foil so that the briquets will have better ventilation. Pile the briquets on the foil, light them and place a rack on top of the pot. When the coals are ready, cook your meal. If the coals get too hot, remove the rack with the meat on it and sprinkle the coals with water or spray them lightly with a spray bottle filled with water. It is best to remove the meat while you're spraying so flying ash doesn't land on it. You can use the flowerpot for grill cooking, stick cooking or direct coal cooking.

Figure 1-18.
Cross section of a
flowerpot grill

Figure 1-19. Flowerpot grill

Newspaper Stove

For low-cost fuel and a quick way to grill hamburgers, a newspaper stove is a great alternative to standard grills. All you need is a 5-gallon garbage can or an ash can, a wire cooling rack, some newspaper and a spray bottle of water. Both types of cans are available at hardware stores.

First, remove the lid of the can. Using 5 sheets of black and white newspaper, gather the paper together, then twist to form small "logs" and place them in the bottom of the can. Repeat this until the can is 1/3 filled, then wad up a single sheet of newspaper and set it on top of the "logs" and light.

Place the cooling rack over the top of the can. Meat that is not more than 3/4 of an inch thick, with some fat content, cooks well on this stove. The fat dripping down on the newspapers keeps them burning. If the flames burn too high, spray them with water to avoid charred, half-cooked food.

Also, you can use the lid of the can to grill simultaneously with the newspaper stove. Just follow the instructions for the garbage can lid grill.

Figure 1-20. Newspaper "logs" in an ash can

Figure 1-21. Newspaper stove

Vertical Spit

If you're looking for a fun and unusual way to cook a chicken or even a turkey outdoors, you may want to try a vertical spit. It works like an outdoor oven; the meat slowly cooks in the pocket of heat created by the vertically placed coals.

To build a vertical spit, you'll need four 3-foot-long metal stakes, a tripod, chicken wire, aluminum foil, heavy string, an oven thermometer and charcoal briquets. Re-bar and metal tubing can be used for the stakes and can be wired together to form a tripod. Both are readily available at hardware stores and can be bought precut to various lengths.

First, drive four metal stakes into the ground to form a square. The distance between the stakes depends on the meat you're cooking. Stakes should be 12 to 14 inches apart for chickens and 24 to 28 inches apart for turkeys. Then cut four pieces of 1-inch mesh chicken wire about 2 feet long and 10 holes wide (cut down the center of the 11th hole). Fasten the long sides of each roll together to make four tubular wire cages. Slip each wire cage over a metal stake, fill each cage with charcoal briquets and light them. You can use briquets that have been presoaked in lighter fluid to facilitate lighting. Be sure not to add any more lighter fluid once the fire is lit because the stream of fluid can catch fire and cause a burst of flames. Also, the flames can be sucked into the lighter fluid can, causing an explosion. You will need to add a few briquets to the wire cages every half hour to maintain a constant temperature. Plan on using about 10 to 15 pounds of briquets. Finally, center the tripod over the four stakes.

Figure 1-22. Stake placement

Figure 1-23. Charcoal briquets in chicken wire cages

Figure 1-24. Tripod placement

Prepare the poultry as if you were cooking it in the oven. To keep the wings from overcooking, tie them close to the body with heavy string. If desired, slip an oven brown-in-bag around the bird to protect it from briquet ashes and to retain juices. Then tie a piece of heavy string or lightweight wire around the legs of the bird. Use a piece long enough so the bird will dangle a few inches above the ground when tied to the top of the tripod. Finally, wrap 18-inch heavy-duty aluminum foil around the outside of the four stakes to hold the heat in an enclosed area.

Figure 1-25. Chicken hanging from the tripod

Figure 1-26. Aluminum foil wrapped around chicken wire cages

Hang an inexpensive oven thermometer by a wire from the tripod at the same level as the bird to help determine the temperature inside the vertical spit. The temperature should be about 325 to 350 degrees. At this temperature, the cooking time for a chicken or turkey is approximately 20 minutes per pound. If the temperature inside the foil square becomes too hot, slide the foil several inches up from the ground or open the foil to allow more circulation of air, which will lower the temperature. If the temperature is lower than 325 to 350 degrees, cook the bird longer. Be sure the temperature doesn't go below 300 degrees if the bird is stuffed, to avoid possible food poisoning. Always use a meat thermometer to check for doneness. For barbecued chicken, slip the oven bag off the bird about 15 minutes before it's done and baste it with your favorite barbecue sauce. If you're not using an oven bag, baste the bird approximately 20 minutes before it is finished cooking. If the chicken browns too quickly, wrap it in foil to stop the browning; it will continue to cook but it won't brown. To simultaneously bake potatoes, place foil-wrapped potatoes on bricks placed on the ground next to the hanging bird. Potatoes will take about one hour to bake this way and need to be turned once after about a half hour.

Figure 1-27. Chicken and potatoes cooking in a vertical spit

Still More Cooking Ideas

You shouldn't let the fact you don't have all of the equipment you need to barbecue stop you from moving outdoors for dinner. There are all sorts of other things you can use to make your barbecue successful, and your guests will remember it for a long time, too. These handy items will make cooking more convenient and more fun.

Shovel Frying Pan

You can transform an everyday shovel into a frying pan or a solid grill for cooking eggs or meats. Just clean a heavy shovel, then cover the metal shovel end with extra-heavy-duty aluminum foil. Use the shovel frying pan by setting it directly on the coals or by propping it on rocks or bricks above the coals.

Figure 1-28. Hamburgers cooking on a shovel frying pan

Pitchfork Skewers

So you don't have enough skewers to cook hot dogs and marshmallows? Never fear—just grab the nearest pitchfork. Sterilize the well-cleaned prongs by placing the pitchfork directly in the hot fire for several minutes. Then cool and wipe it off, and it's ready to use. You may even wish to buy a pitchfork just for cookouts. No one will forget your party when you whip out hot dogs on a pitchfork.

Figure 1-29. Pitchfork skewers

Figure 1-30. Pitchfork skewers and shovel frying pan used over open coals

CHAPTER 2

FIRE

S pending time sitting around a campfire watching the embers glow is a calming and wonderful way to spend an evening in the wild. However, if you can't get to the woods to build a campfire, having a cookout in your own backyard can evoke some of the same feelings, especially when hot, delicious food is part of the bargain.

A hardwood fire is ideal for cooking, but most people don't have the facilities to build one in the backyard, so the next best thing is charcoal briquets. The small pillow-shaped coals provide a steady heat suitable for outdoor cooking. Try two or three different brands until you find the one you like best. Remember that you generally get what you pay for and the most inexpensive brand may not always be the best bargain. Whatever brand you choose, the more you use it, the better you will be able to control the heat and anticipate how long it will take to cook your food.

There are a few things you need to be aware of with briquets. NEVER use charcoal briquets indoors. NEVER use gasoline to light briquets because the fumes are highly explosive; always use a charcoal lighter fluid or other method specially designed for this purpose.

Preparing the Area

The first step in getting ready for a backyard barbecue is to select the cooking area. You'll want to barbecue on a level, open area at least six feet from flammable materials such as buildings, shrubs, dry grass, wood or overhanging branches.

If you're going to start your fire with charcoal briquets on dirt, sand or gravel, you may also want to put down a layer of heavy-duty aluminum foil first. Foil will keep the charcoal from becoming imbedded in the sand or dirt, and it also helps to maintain the air circulation necessary for a good fire. If you have a commercial charcoal barbecue, you can build a charcoal briquet fire right in the bowl of the grill. Hibachis and kettle grills have charcoal pans that allow air circulation underneath.

Starting Charcoal Briquets

Nothing puts a damper on a party as quickly as charcoal briquets that won't start. Hungry guests gathering around the grill expecting sizzling steaks aren't going to want to wait 20 or 30 minutes for the charcoal to heat before the steaks can even be placed on the grill. Make sure you have a tried-and-true method for starting the briquets before you plan a party. Here are a few ideas that should help you find the method you like best.

Lighter Fluid

The most common method for starting charcoal briquets is to pile them into a pyramid and soak them with lighter fluid or charcoal starter. Let the fluid-saturated briquets sit for 3 or 4 minutes before you light them. Then place a lighted match onto the briquets. After burning for approximately 5 to 10 minutes, the fire will burn down, but the charcoal will continue to heat. You will know that the briquets are heating properly when white ash begins to form around the edges. It will take 20 to 40 minutes before the briquets are ready for cooking. The time depends on the type of briquets, the lighter fluid, and the amount of wind. DON'T add more lighter fluid once the flame goes out, because if a flame is still in the briquets, it could flare up into the can and cause an explosion. Instead, be sure to douse the briquets thoroughly with lighter fluid before you light them. Once the briquets are ready, use tongs to spread them over the cooking surface.

Electric Starter

If you prefer, you can buy an electric starter at most hardware stores. This is a circular metal device that you plug into an electrical outlet. You place it in the center of a pyramid-shaped stack of briquets, and the coals nearest the heating coil will become hot first. Leave the electric starter in place until the briquets are ready.

Charcoal Marinating Can

You can buy charcoal briquets that have been soaked in a flammable substance to make them light quickly, but they cost more than your average charcoal. If you do a lot of barbecuing, you may want to set up your own marinating can. Take a clean one-gallon can and fill it with charcoal briquets. Then pour lighter fluid over them until they are covered and place a lid on the can. Let them stand overnight, or allow them to "marinate" until they cease to bubble. At this point they are fully marinated. When cooking with marinated briquets, use a mixture of half-marinated and half-dry briquets. Stack them alternately in a pyramid, then light. Add more briquets to the "marinade" for your next barbecue and add lighter fluid. Then place a tight-fitting lid over the can and place it in an area where it will not be a fire hazard.

If you're not having your picnic in the backyard, you may want to take just a few marinated briquets with you in a sealed plastic bag. Wrap the bag in a piece of heavy-duty foil. When you arrive at the area where you are going to build the fire, simply open up the foil, remove the briquets from the bag, place them on the foil and light.

Chimney Can

Figure 2-1. Chimney can

You can turn a clean one-gallon can into a "chimney can" that will start charcoal briquets with the help of newspapers. Cut out the bottom of an empty can and place it on the cooking surface. Wad up several newspapers and place them in the can. Then pile several briquets on top of the papers. Place a rock underneath one edge of the can to provide a draft area, then light the newspaper. If you have problems, fan a paper plate at the bottom where you have propped up the can. This will help air circulate enough to fire up the charcoal briquets. Once the briquets are lit, you can lift the can away from them with a pair of pliers and the briquets will spread out, ready for cooking. This method is very successful with marinated briquets.

Commercial Chimney Starter

A quick and easy method of getting briquets started is by using a commercial chimney starter. Simply wad up newspaper and place it below the metal divider in the bottom of the starter. Next, pile the briquets on top of the divider. Because there are holes around the paper area and between the paper and the briquets, there is a built-in draft system. Just light the newspaper, and in no time at all the briquets will be ready. Hold the chimney starter by its handle and pour the briquets into your grill—this is a surefire, no-mess way to get the cooking started.

Figure 2-2. Commercial chimney starter

Speed Up the Briquets

If you find your briquets are taking their sweet time and aren't ready for cooking when you are, speed up the heating process by carefully using one of the following methods:

- **Hair dryer**—A portable hair dryer is one of the best ways of speeding up the charcoal briquets' preparation time. The hot air is forced across the briquets, causing them to glow with a light flame. This will spread the heat throughout the briquets almost instantly. Briquets can be heated in about 15 to 20 minutes using this method. One warning, though—you'll want to keep plastic hair dryers away from the intense heat; they melt.

Figure 2-3. Hair dryer used to speed up the briquets' preparation time

- **Bellows**—A fireplace bellows can be used to speed the heating process.
- **Paper plate**—If you don't have access to any of these other methods, just fan the briquets with a paper plate or frisbee.

Flavor Fun

To add a little extra flavor to whatever you're cooking, try burning something aromatic on the coals. Hickory chips or fruitwood add to the aroma and flavor. You can buy these chips commercially. To use, just follow the directions on the package. If you feel particularly innovative, experiment with sprinkling various herbs on the coals.

Controlling the Heat

The briquets will be a glowing white when they are ready for cooking. In the evening they will appear to be red. A briquet that is not quite hot enough will have a black area in its center. Once they are glowing, spread out the briquets so that you can begin cooking with them. The real key to cooking with briquets is learning how to control the heat. You can adjust the temperature by rearranging the briquets or by changing the distance of the rack from the glowing briquets.

A simple way to judge the temperature of a fire is to place your hand above the charcoal briquets at about the height at which your food will cook. If you can only count one to two seconds before having to move your hand, you have a very hot fire of about 400 to 500 degrees. If you can leave your hand there for three to four seconds, you have a hot fire of about 300 to 400 degrees. Meat will be more tender if it is cooked over a fire that is 300 to 400 degrees. For blackening foods such as Cajun fish, use a very hot fire.

To make a very hot fire, place the briquets side by side, touching. For a hot fire, arrange the briquets in a checkerboard pattern, leaving a charcoal-sized space between each briquet. This is the kind of fire you'll need if you're cooking with a pan. Be sure to check your food while it is cooking to see that the heat isn't too intense.

As charcoal briquets burn down, they will form a white ash on the outside, which also causes them to cool. If you need more heat from them, tap the briquets lightly with a pair of tongs. This will cause the ash to fall off and the coal to become hotter. As the briquets burn down, move them closer together to increase the heat.

Multitemperature Grilling

As we all know, different foods require different cooking temperatures. To avoid overcooking and undercooking food due to a one-temperature grill, create various heat settings to accommodate all of your temperature needs. Simply divide your grill into three sections or "settings." In the first section, place the briquets so they are touching one another—this will be your "high" setting. Follow the checkerboard pattern in the second section for your "medium" setting. And finally, place the briquets a few inches apart in the third section to create your "low" setting. This will ensure that all of your recipes are cooked to perfection.

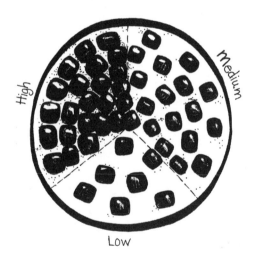

Figure 2-4. Multitemperature grilling briquet placement

Adding Briquets

When adding briquets to a well-established bed of briquets, place them at the edges. Adding them to the center will immediately reduce the heat. If you are cooking a large piece of meat that has a long cooking time, such as a turkey or a roast, keep adding the briquets to the edges and push them toward the center as they burn down.

Controlling Flare-ups

One of the biggest problems people have while cooking meat over charcoal briquets is controlling flare-ups. They're caused by grease dripping onto the coals and catching fire. The flames blacken the food that's cooking, which makes it look and taste unappealing. A good way to avoid flare-ups is to trim as much fat as possible from meat, and buy extra-lean hamburger. You may also want to use a spray bottle full of water to control flare-ups as they occur; a squirt gun is also very effective. If you have a grill with a lid, cover the grill and close the vents to control flare-ups. Remember, however, that you don't want to cool the charcoal—you only want to control the flames.

Another tip: If you have some iceberg lettuce around, drop some of the outer leaves of the lettuce onto the areas that flare up. Iceberg lettuce is about 95 percent moisture and will suffocate a flare-up. Table salt will also douse the flames.

Reusing Charcoal Briquets

Most people don't reuse charcoal, they just let it burn out and throw it away after one use. Briquets can be used two to three times if they are doused or extinguished as soon as you are through cooking with them.

There are several ways to stop briquets from burning. One is to douse them with water or place them in water with a pair of tongs. If water is used to douse burning briquets, dry them out completely before you reuse them. On dome grills, put on the lid and close all vents to smother the briquets. Briquets that have already been used should not be placed back into a charcoal marinating can, because they will disintegrate and settle on the bottom. When using briquets for the second or third time, add them to the top of the briquet pyramid.

Gas Barbecues

One alternative to using briquets is to turn to a commercial gas grill. Depending on the type of gas barbecue you have, there are several ways to regulate the heat. Most models have control knobs with high, medium and low settings. The high setting is about 500 degrees; medium, 400 degrees; and low, 300 degrees. You can check the exact temperature of your gas grill by buying an oven thermometer at the grocery store. Place the thermometer in the center of the rack and close the lid for ten minutes, then read. Grill lids can be closed to create an oven effect. If you want to adjust the temperature in the "oven," just use the control knobs.

CHAPTER 3

ACCESSORIES

N ow that you've picked out your grill and the fire is burning, there are a few other things you may want to have around to help you organize your backyard barbecue and make the occasion a lot easier on yourself.

Getting Organized

Having all of your tools and utensils at your fingertips will prevent you from running in and out of the house during your cookout. Getting organized is simple and inexpensive.

Hanging Equipment Bag

Buy a hanging shoe or lingerie organizer with see-through pockets at the store. You can use the pockets to store everything you'll need. Separate paper plates, napkins, eating utensils, cups and cooking utensils into individual pockets. Grilling equipment with handles can be hung over the hanger portion of the bag. When you're not using the bag, you can hang it in the kitchen, utility closet or even the garage, and it's easy to transfer to an outdoor hook or a tree branch when you're ready to fire

Figure 3-1. Equipment bag suspended from a tree

up the grill. And if a thunderstorm is a surprise guest at your outdoor dinner, you can pack up in just minutes.

Lunch or Tackle Box

An old lunch box or a fishing tackle box can easily be turned into a handy storage box for your barbecue paraphernalia. You can use the space to store all of your spices and barbecue sauces, as well as pot holders, utensils and other items you might need. Both lunch and tackle boxes come in various sizes, so look around to find one that suits your needs.

Plastic Cleaning Container

You may want to make a stop at the housewares department of your local store and pick up a plastic cleaning container. These durable containers have handles and are divided into compartments, so it will be easy to organize utensils and spices and have them ready anytime you need them.

Carpenter's Apron

If you would rather have all of your necessities at your fingertips, buy a carpenter's apron for yourself. The large front pockets provide plenty of space for all of the tools you'll need for your outdoor experience.

Serving Accessories

If you don't have a picnic table or a patio set, don't worry. There are plenty of other ways to serve your food outdoors with ease if you think creatively.

Ironing Board Buffet

Your ironing board has probably been relegated to just the task of ironing in the past, but you don't need to limit its uses. It can also serve as a portable buffet or a table for equipment when you're barbecuing. Place the ironing board on a level, solid surface, and check to make sure it's secure before you use it. To make the board more stable, place bricks or bags of sand on its legs. Then drape a tablecloth or oilcloth over the board, and it's ready for any outdoor serving ideas you can think of. For those of you who are a bit more ambitious, you can make a table drape with pockets to hold all of the utensils. This can be simply sewn and puts all of the utensils at your guests' fingertips.

Figure 3-2. Ironing board buffet

Salad Bar and Soda Pop Station

Keeping salads and drinks cold can be a problem outdoors, but there is an easy solution. Take a laundry basket, a plastic baby tub, a wheelbarrow, a wagon or even a child's plastic wading pool and fill with ice cubes. Place soda cans in the ice around the outer edges of the container. Then place the salad bowls in the middle of the container. The most secure way to place the bowl is to make an indentation in the ice with your hand, then place the bowl in and twist it side to side.

Figure 3-3. Wheelbarrow salad bar

Figure 3-4. Laundry basket soda pop station

Figure 3-5. Wagon salad bar

Ice Bowl

Another way to keep food cold for a long period of time is to use a block of ice. Place the ice on a large tray or pan, or directly on the ground. Chip out a hollow on the top of the ice just slightly smaller than the bowl that will contain the food you want to keep cold. Then fill a metal bowl with hot water and slide it around the hollow on top of the ice block until the bowl fits into the ice. You may need to change the hot water more than once. When the food is in the bowl, the solid ice counter will hold the food and keep it cool for a long period of time.

Double Boiler Food Keeper

If you've got a double boiler on hand, you can put ice in the bottom pan, and then put the food you want to keep cool in the top pan. Keep the pan covered with a lid when you aren't serving. It's a great idea for chilled salads.

To keep foods warm while serving, heat rock salt in your oven and place it in the bottom of a double boiler. Then place the food you want to keep warm in the top pan and put the lid on. This works well if you want to fix the food before your guests arrive.

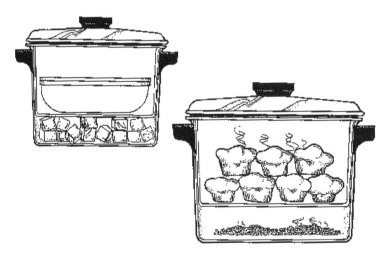

Figure 3-6. Double boiler food keeper

Ice for Punch

Keeping punch cool can be a problem, but chill out. Colorful ice rings for your punch bowl will not only keep the drinks cool, they will add elegance. You can add maraschino cherries, berries, pineapple, mint or other leaves,

Figure 3-7. Floral ice rings

or small flowers to your ice ring to make it interesting. If you use flowers, make sure they are not poisonous. You can create contrast by adding food coloring to the water you're freezing.

To make an ice ring, gather the fruit or other decorations you plan to use along with an interestingly shaped pan. Bundt pans, gelatin molds, or even plastic cups for smaller ice cubes all make good molds. Arrange the decorations in the bottom of the pan upside down so they will look natural when you turn the molded ice over. Then pour a shallow layer of water into the pan; stop pouring before the decorations are completely covered and begin to float. Place in the freezer for one to two hours, until the water has frozen. This will set the decorations in place. Then add water to just below the rim of the mold, allowing space for the water to expand as it freezes. Then freeze again.

To have a multicolored ice ring, tint the first layer one color, then add a different food color to each new layer. Make sure each layer is completely frozen before you add the next, or the colors will run together.

Some other party ice ideas include freezing tiny decorations in regular ice cubes. Freezing fruit juices, or the punch itself, to form your ice ring or cubes adds flavor instead of diluting your punch as the ice melts. Whatever kind of ice you choose, you should freeze your ice ring a day or two before the party to help cut down on the time you'll spend on last-minute preparations.

Halloween Hands

Why not add some frightful delight to your next Halloween party with this "hands-on" project? Thoroughly wash out the inside of a pair of latex surgical gloves—or turn them inside-out—and fill them with water. Tie the ends securely and place them in the freezer overnight. When frozen, remove the gloves and place the ice "hands" in the punch bowl. All the spooks will love this ghoulishly cool treat.

Frisbee Plate Holder

There usually aren't quite enough tables to go around when eating outside, and we've all had to deal with the dilemma of falling or leaking food because of a soggy paper plate, so here's a solution. Inexpensive paper plates fit very nicely into most frisbees. The frisbee gives support to the paper plate and allows you to cut your food easily. When you're planning on serving several courses, place that many paper plates in the frisbee. Each time a course is finished, simply have your guests peel off the used plate, and voila! You're ready for the next course. Frisbees also provide a splash of color to your party.

Tablecloth Tips

Speaking of tables, Mother Nature is always a guest at our outdoor dinners, and that can make for some interesting dining. In fact, airborne paper plates and napkins are as much a part of eating outdoors as ants at a picnic.

Windproof Tablecloth

Instead of placing rocks on each person's place setting when the breeze blows, why not try a pretty, windproof solution, and make your own picnic tablecloth with special pockets to hold each place setting? An example is a cloth with pockets shaped like strawberries. Each strawberry has a large pocket for the plate, one loop on the left side for the fork and two loops on the right side for the spoon and knife. Slipping those supplies into the pockets and anchoring paper cups with ice cubes will keep your eating utensils on the table where they belong.

Figure 3-8. Windproof tablecloth

Sandbag Weights

To keep your tablecloth in place, sew tiny two-inch-square bags from scraps of cloth and fill the bags with sand or pebbles. Attach each bag to a clothespin by threading yarn through the clothespin's metal coil and then sewing the end of the yarn to the sandbag. Snap the clothespin-sandbags to the edges of your tablecloth on windy days.

Drapery Weights

Sewing drapery weights into the hem of your tablecloth is another way to prevent it from flying away in the breeze. Drapery weights can be purchased at most fabric stores. If you can't find drapery weights—when you throw out your old plastic shower curtain, save the weights from the hem and use them to anchor your tablecloth.

Insect Control

Unfortunately, there are usually at least a few uninvited guests who show up at any outdoor meal. Flies, ants, wasps and mosquitoes all want the right to dine alongside you, or even on you. But with a little planning, there are ways to discourage the bugs.

Commercial Methods

One way to prevent bugs from invading a party is to spray the party area with insect spray that is made specially for yards and decks. When you spray the repellent in the air, it settles to the ground and kills the insects in the sprayed area. These sprays repel bugs for up to four hours and work much better than spraying body repellent in the air. To avoid food contamination, be sure to read the manufacturer's instructions to find out how long before the party you should spray. It's also nice to have regular insect repellent available for your guests, too. Another important tip: Don't water your lawn the day of the party. Water always attracts bugs.

Also, citronella insect repellent candles can be bought at any grocery store. These candles not only add a warm ambience to your party, they also make the insects bug off!

Lights

To add a decorative touch and get rid of pests too, you may want to use Christmas lights to brighten an evening party. Colored lights, especially yellow ones, don't attract bugs as much as white lights do, so you are actually discouraging the insects while creating an atmosphere for a festive evening.

Embroidery-Hoop Lid

One of my favorite solutions for keeping flies off serving dishes before and during an outdoor feast is to use the embroidery-hoop technique. Simply tear off a piece of plastic wrap and fasten it between the two hoops as if it were a piece of cloth to be stitched. Place the hoops over plates and bowls and you will prevent flies from enjoying the food before you do—and you'll keep the food from drying out as well.

Figure 3-9. Embroidery hoops and plastic wrap used to keep insects off food

Net Table Cover

If you want to keep the little critters away from your entire table, here's an easy tip. Set the table and then cover it completely with colorful nylon netting which remains in place until guests come to the table. Inexpensive netting is available up to 72 inches in width, it's washable, and the food looks pretty through it, too.

Fans

When you are working to prepare food for cooking, insects are especially unwelcome helpers. So set up your work table with two large fans facing each other. Turn the fans on high. This will not only help keep the insects off the food, but it will make it much cooler for you to work. When the food is ready, put a fan on one end of the serving table to keep the bugs away.

Figure 3-10. Fan used to keep serving table insect-free

Good Clean Fun

Keeping the little ones, as well as the grownups, clean during an outdoor adventure can be a problem. Here are some ideas that will wipe away your worries.

Soap Bottle Cleaner

If you don't want people tracking the outdoors inside every time they need to wash their hands, here's a solution. All you need to keep hands clean is an empty dish soap squirt bottle. Fill it with water, add a dash of liquid soap and then squeeze the solution out as needed for cleaning messy hands.

Outdoor Dressing Room

If you want to keep the kids from tracking dirt into your house during your next pool or sprinkler party, just construct an instant outdoor dressing room. All you need is a large, sturdy umbrella with a hook handle, two shower curtains and a tree branch.

Open the umbrella and suspend it from a branch so it hangs about six feet off the ground. If your branch is too high, fear not. Tie the umbrella to the branch using a piece of rope. Slip the holes of the first shower curtain over the tips of the umbrella ribs (the holes and the ribs are spaced exactly the same distance apart). Continue around the umbrella with the second shower curtain and overlap the last two holes to create a door. In minutes you will have a changing room that is just as easy to take down as it was to put up.

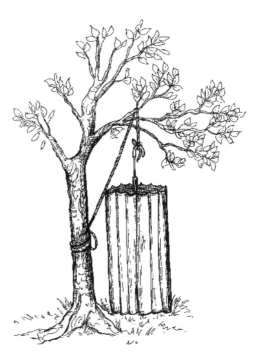

Figure 3-11. Outdoor dressing room

By using the outdoor dressing room instructions, you can also make a portable playhouse for the kids. For windows, cut two squares out of the front of the curtain. To make the glass for the windows, sew or glue a piece of clear plastic into each cut-out square. Use black electrical tape to make window panes. Finally, stencil flowers on the bottom edge of the curtain to create a garden. Not only is this playhouse terrific for a backyard party, but it is also mobile enough to take with you to the park.

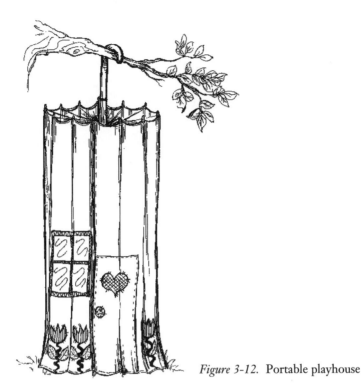

Figure 3-12. Portable playhouse

Decorations

Decorations make a party look as festive as it feels. Get the whole family involved in making your decorations—the job gets done a lot quicker and it allows your family to spend time together. Not only do you want your food to look nice, you also want the backyard to be inviting, and there's a way to do that without going to a lot of trouble or expense.

Paper-Bag Lanterns
Just buy some lunch-sized paper bags and fill each of them with an inch or two of sand or a cup of rock salt. Light votive candles and use tongs to set one in the middle of the sand or salt in each bag. Assembling the lanterns on a cookie sheet allows you to easily carry them to their destination. Bag lanterns make great lights for entryways and patios, and they will burn for hours.

Firecracker Candles

Firecracker candles are a fun way to add a little life to your table. Using the open end of a one-pound coffee can, press down on a piece of Styrofoam to cut out a circle. Push the circular piece of Styrofoam to the bottom of the can. Center a candle in the can by pushing it into the foam at the bottom of the can and light it. Make sure the candle is at least 3 inches longer than the height of the can. Drop a few pieces of dry ice into the can and pour hot water over them. Firecracker candles will give your event a big bang, and you've created a unique effect from everyday household items.

Maypole Centerpiece

Creating a maypole centerpiece adds elegance to any table. Place a thick dowel or the center pole from an artificial Christmas tree into a brick with holes so that it stands upright. Attach wide ribbon or streamers to the top of the pole and weave them around the pole until they cover the top 8 inches (the ribbon should be a few feet longer than the pole). Spread the ends of the ribbon out at the base of the pole and tape them near the edge of the table. This will form a circle around the pole. Then, insert ivy and flowers under the ribbon that is woven around the pole. If you are using a Christmas tree pole, simply insert the flowers into the holes that the branches would normally go in. Fasten a ribbon to the top of the pole for added elegance. Finally, place your serving bowls over the ribbon where it is taped down. This serving setup is perfect for more formal backyard dining.

Fruit Swizzle Sticks

If you want to add a little fun and flavor to cold beverages, fruit swizzle sticks will do the job. Alternate fruit on a swizzle stick or bamboo skewer; grapes, cherries and strawberries work well. Add a lemon wedge to the bottom of the stick and place a swizzle stick in each glass. This is a terrific way to dress up a drink—and your guests will have something to munch on, too.

Helium Balloons

Helium balloons add color and fun to any outdoor festivity. They are terrific for theme parties, such as the Fourth of July, and are relatively inexpensive. To keep the balloons from flying away, anchor them by tying the ends of the strings to a rock.

You'll really impress your guests if they walk through a balloon arch to get to the backyard. First, tie the end of a piece of fishing line to a chair. Then, fill up helium balloons and tie them. Make sets of two balloons by fastening the knots together with a paper clip. Next, take two sets of two balloons, fasten them together and attach them to the fishing line with string or masking tape. Continue attaching sets of four balloons to the fishing line until the arch is the desired length. Tie the loose end of the line to another chair, and as the helium lifts the balloons toward the sky, an arch will form.

If you don't want to rent a helium tank, you can achieve the look of helium balloons without the helium. Inflate regular balloons and use masking tape to attach them to a dowel. Cover several dowels completely with balloons. Then stick the ends of the dowels in a piece of Styrofoam in the bottom of a large flowerpot. The arrangement makes the balloons look like they are floating, but you didn't have to use helium.

Fruit Totem Pole

A fruit totem pole adds pizzazz and color to any festivity. All you need is a honeydew melon and seven other pieces of fruit of different colors (a grapefruit, an orange, a red apple, a green apple, a pear, a lemon and a lime), a dowel with pointy ends and a two-foot-long cord. Place the melon on a table and wrap the cord around its base to keep it from rolling. Push the dowel

Figure 3-13. Fruit totem pole

through the middle of the melon so it is sticking straight up. Then push the next smallest piece of fruit (grapefruit) through the dowel so it is on top of the melon. Continue to add fruit to the dowel, decreasing in size as you move upward, until you have created a totem pole with the smallest piece of fruit at the top. Decorate each piece of fruit with a paper face and symbols.

Edible Centerpiece

An edible centerpiece is a beautiful and creative way to serve raw veggies. Line the sides and the bottom of a large basket with a handle with Romaine lettuce. Then arrange ready-to-eat vegetables on top of the bed of lettuce—cauliflower flanked by two wedges of red cabbage, hollowed-out green peppers filled with carrot sticks, five bunches of radishes with their bottoms trimmed and whole mushrooms. Use cherry tomatoes and cucumber slices to fill in any gaps in your centerpiece. Lastly, wire bunches of scallions to the basket's handle and embellish them with parsley bouquets and radishes cut to look like flowers. Serve the salad dressings, croutons and other salad ingredients in flowerpots lined with plastic wrap. This centerpiece looks almost too good to eat!

CHAPTER 4

GRILL
COOKING

T he smell of meat cooking on the grill brings the idea of outdoor parties to mind like no other. There are several types
of grills available for preparing your meals: wire, solid or
hinged basket.

The most common kind of grill is the wire grill that comes with
a commercial barbecue. The best kind of wire grill can be raised
or lowered to regulate the heat and is large enough to cook for several people. If you want to improvise your own barbecue, an oven
rack, cookie cooling rack or even a heavy screen can be used for
the grill. Some racks, like oven racks, have wires too far apart for
grilling hamburgers, but they work well for grilling steaks or other
large items. A cookie cooling rack, which has more narrow spaces
between its wires, can be placed on top of the oven rack to allow
you to cook both large and small items.

If you are interested in preparing quick side dishes or perhaps a
pancake breakfast on the grill, you may want to use a solid grill or

Figure 4-1. Small-holed grilling rack used in a gas grill

griddle. Using a solid grill is like cooking in a frying pan, only it has a much greater surface.

Another option when it comes to grilling is the hinged wire basket. It comes in all shapes and sizes; some baskets are large enough to hold three to four pieces of chicken or a large steak. You can even buy a basket made especially for fish. Baskets are great for controlled cooking of odd-shaped food. You can suspend the basket over the coals by placing a brick under each side. Also available to buy are grill racks with small holes. This kind of rack allows you to cook food as small as diced vegetables.

Beating the Heat

The key to cooking over a grill is learning how to use the grill to regulate heat. Heat is controlled over coals by changing the placement of your grilling rack. The farther the grill is away from the coals, the slower the food will cook. The average distance between the food and the coals should be about four inches. If you have a thicker piece of meat which needs to be well done, it should be moved farther away from the coals so it cooks more slowly and thoroughly. Food that is thin can cook faster and can be moved closer to the source of the heat. The cut of the meat, its size and shape and the temperature of the coals will affect the time it takes to cook your food.

Commercial kettle grills and hibachis have air vents at the bottom to regulate the amount of oxygen circulating around the coals. By closing the vents, you cut off oxygen and decrease the heat; opening the vents increases the heat.

Grilling Meats

Grill cooking is a dry-heat method. Less-tender cuts of meat do not become more tender on the grill like they would with a more moist method of cooking, so you will want to use tender cuts of meat, ground meat patties, or less-tender cuts of meat that have been marinated or tenderized before you grill them.

Here are some ideas of the cuts of meat you may want to use the next time you're ready to fire up the grill.

Beef Cuts

Filet mignon or tenderloin steak
Top sirloin steak
Porterhouse steak
T-bone steak
Spencer or rib-eye steak

Rib steak
Blade chuck steak
Ground beef patties
New York or strip steak
Marinated cuts, such as flank steak, top round, and skirt steak rolls

Pork Cuts

Country-style spareribs
Regular spareribs
Ham slices

Back ribs
Pork tenderloin
Center-cut leg steak
Pork chops, including loin chop, rib chop, sirloin chop or blade chop

Other

Whole fish or fillets
Chicken parts

Turkey parts

Grilling Tips

There are some things you can do to make sure grilled food is cooked properly.

- Trim excess fat from the meat cuts to eliminate flare-ups, and use extra-lean hamburger.
- Thin steaks and chops will sometimes curl around the edges. Clipping the fat in about 1/2-inch deep along the edges will eliminate this.
- Use tongs to turn a steak instead of a fork. A fork punches holes into the meat and allows the juices to run out.
- Brush food with oil before placing it on the grill so that it doesn't stick to the grill. Canola and vegetable oils are the best. Or before lighting the grill, spray it with nonstick cooking spray; this method is less fattening.
- Check to see if a steak is done by making a thin cut in the center. The best way to check for doneness is by using a meat thermometer. Depending on how you like your steak, here are the guidelines that should be followed: medium/rare = 145 degrees, medium = 160 degrees, well done = 170 degrees.

Arm Test

Here's a clever way to tell if your steak is done. Touch the meat with your fingers and gently press down. Then turn your arm so your thumb is facing up. Press down on your wrist, the middle of your forearm and the fleshy area at your elbow. If the meat feels like your wrist, it is well done. If it feels like your forearm, it is medium and if it feels like your soft elbow area, it is medium rare.

Marinating or Tenderizing Meats: A Matter of Taste

If you are going to grill less-tender cuts of meat, you will probably want to tenderize or marinate them before cooking. Marinating adds seasoning and moisture to meats, which makes them more flavorful and tender. You can also physically tenderize the meat or use a commercial tenderizer. When meats are physically tenderized, tough cuts are ground up whole and Swiss-steak cuts are often scored by a commercial machine to break up meat fibers. At home, you can tenderize your steaks by pounding them with a mallet specially designed for that purpose, or by pounding them with the side of a nonbreakable plate. You may choose to use a commercial meat tenderizer on flavorful, less-tender cuts of meat. Sprinkle the meat lightly and evenly on all sides with either a seasoned or unseasoned meat tenderizer. Tenderizer comes in a shaker jar and looks like salt, or it may come in liquid form. Follow package directions closely for best results.

In marinades, the vinegar mixed with oil works chemically to make meat more tender. The meat is submerged in the marinade for the specified time so that the meat has time to become tender and soak up the flavor of the marinade. Marinating meats should be kept in the refrigerator.

One handy way to marinate meat is to place it in a self-sealing plastic bag, pour the marinade into the bag over the meat, then place the bag in a bowl or on a plate in your refrigerator. Be sure the marinade covers at least half of the meat. One advantage to this method is that you don't need to use as much marinade. Turn the bag at least three or four times; a good habit is to turn the meat every time you open your refrigerator.

Now that you have read this section, you're ready to fire up the grill for your backyard party. Turn to the recipe section of the book for fantastic grilling and marinade recipes you'll surely want to try.

CHAPTER 5

SMOKE COOKING

T he unique taste and aroma of smoke cooking is the ultimate outdoor experience. The smell of hickory in the air is enough to get anyone's taste buds working overtime. Smoke cooking is surprisingly easy because there is very little maintenance required once the cooking begins. Along with the many different woods to choose from in order to get different flavors, there are also different ways in which to do the actual smoking.

The Charcoal Smoker

You're already a pro at getting charcoal briquets started and keeping them hot, so this will be a cinch of a smoker to use at your next backyard party. The charcoal smoker is made of metal and consists of a charcoal pan, a water pan, a grill rack and a dome-shaped lid. Contrary to what you may think, a smoker does not give off a lot of smoke, but you should be careful to use it on a nonflammable surface and also to use a drip pan underneath it.

Figure 5-1. Charcoal smoker

Getting Started

First, for easy clean-up when you're done, you should line the charcoal and water pans with heavy-duty aluminum foil—make sure you poke a hole in the bottom of the foil in the charcoal pan to allow for air circulation. If you line the two pans with foil, clean-up will take no time at all. Next, fill the charcoal pan with briquets. As with any store-bought cooking equipment, be sure to follow the manufacturer's instructions for the amount of charcoal per pound of meat that you will need; you should always use at least five pounds. You can use any of the techniques we've already discussed to get your charcoal burning. If you are cooking a large piece of meat that may require additional briquets, make sure you light the extras a good half hour before they are needed so your cooking never comes to a standstill. Next, place the wood on top of the briquets. Keep in mind that one wood chunk generally equals a handful of wood chips. As you experiment with different amounts of wood, you will find the amount that suits your taste, but generally one chunk or one handful of chips is a good amount to start with. Remember that wood chunks give a longer lasting smoke than wood chips. There are several very important things you need to know about the wood in order to get the taste you desire. First, you should always use either "green" wood (freshly cut) or wood that has soaked in water for an hour before you are ready to use it. It is important to soak dry wood to insure that the wood will smoke—not burn. Also, you should always use wood from a deciduous tree, NOT from an evergreen. The resin in evergreen wood will destroy the look and the taste of your food. Second, there are many different woods to choose from and each will give you a different flavor. Some very popular woods are hickory, mesquite, palmetto, cherry, apple and walnut. Fruit and nut woods are readily available, and you will have fun trying the various kinds to decide on your favorite.

The next step is to put insulated mitts on and place the water pan into the smoker and fill it with warm tap water (hot water should be used if the temperature outside is below 50 degrees). Then, place the food in a single layer on the grill, cover, and let the smoke cooking begin. If you are cooking for a period of several hours, you may have to add water to the pan. Today, most smokers come with an access door through which you can check the pan and add water as necessary. When adding water, make sure you use a nonflammable container with a long spout so that your hand doesn't get too close to the heat. A metal watering can works very well for this.

Figure 5-2. Meat on charcoal smoker's grill rack

Cooking Time

Here are some general times for smoke cooking:

QUICK GLANCE COOK GUIDE

ALWAYS FILL WATER PAN WITH APPROXIMATELY 5-1/2 QUARTS HOT WATER FROM TAP UNLESS RECIPE INDICATES OTHER MEASUREMENT.

Food and Weight	Amount of Charcoal	Amount of Wood Chunks	Temperature or Test for Doneness*	Smoke Cooking Time(Hours)	Number of Servings Per lb.
BEEF, Venison or Other Game Animal Boneless Roasts					
3-4 lbs.	level	1	140 degree F rare	3-4	3-4
5-7 lbs.	level full	1	160 degree F medium	5-6	
8-10 lbs.	heaping	2	170 degree F well	7-9**	
CHICKEN					
Fryers(2-2 1/2 lbs. ea.)			180 degree F or		
1 to 3 whole, split or cut up	rounded	1	leg will move easily in	4-5	3-4
Roasters (5 lbs.) 1 or 2	rounded to heaping		socket	6-8	3-4
FISH					
Fillets, full grill	level	1	flakes when	2-3	3-4
Steaks	level	1-2	forked	2-3	
Whole Pan Fish	level	1-2		2-3	
Whole, large, 6 lb.	rounded	1-2		3-5	
GAME					
Small birds (dove, quail, squab, pheasant, duck)	rounded	2	leg will move easily in socket	3-5	1 to 3
HAM					
Cooked, all sizes	level	1-2	130 degree F	3-5	3-4
Fresh, 10 lb.	heaping	2-3	170 degree F	7-10**	
LAMB			140 degree F rare		
Leg or shoulder roasts 5-7 lb.	rounded	1-2	160 degree F rare 175 degree F done	5-7**	3-4
LOBSTER TAILS	level to	1-2	flesh white and	1-2	2
Full grill	rounded		firm		
PORK					
Chops, 6-8 lb. (1" thk)	rounded	1	170 degree F	3-4	3-4
Roasts, 3-5 lb.	rounded	1	170 degree F	5-7	
Roasts, 5-7 lb.	heaping	2	170 degree F	7-8**	2
Ribs, 5 lb.	rounded	1-2	well done, meat pulls away from bone	4-6	
SAUSAGE					
Links, full grill	level to rounded	1-2	well done, 170 degree F for cook before eating pork sausage	3-5 for cook before eating	3-4
SHRIMP	level	1	flesh white and firm	1-2	3
TURKEY (Unstuffed)			180 degree F or		
8-12 lb.	level	2	leg will move	7-9**	2-3
13-20 lb.	heaping	2-3	easily in socket	10-12**	

* Temperatures are those recommended by the food industries for consumer use.
** When cooking very large pieces of food: Your Outdoor Smoker can cook up to about 5-6 hours on a pan of charcoal. Turkeys or cuts of meat over 6 to 8 lbs. could take longer to cook. If you are going to cook large pieces of food, you will need to add more charcoal and water during the cooking period. Smoke Cooking Times are approximate. NOTE: ELECTRIC COOKING TIMES COULD BE SHORTER THAN THOSE SHOWN ON CHART.

Chart courtesy of Meco Corporation, Greenville, TN

Many variables affect the cooking time, so it is important to always use a meat thermometer to determine whether the meat is done. Smoked meats will look different when they have finished cooking than meats that are grilled or cooked in your oven, so be sure to use a thermometer. Also, make sure the meat is completely thawed before you begin to smoke cook it. Air temperature, elevation, humidity, type of charcoal and mass and weight of the food will all factor into your cooking time. And most important of all to remember: Every time you lift the lid of the smoker, you have to add at least 15 minutes to your cooking time. If you want to check whether the smoker is working, hold your hand several inches away from the smoker across from the charcoal pan. If you feel heat, you're still cooking. Only lift the lid to add more charcoal or to use the meat thermometer to check for doneness. When the meat is ready but your guests aren't, don't panic. The meat can stay warm and moist in the smoker if you baste it with juice from the water pan and wrap it in foil.

Other Uses for Your Smoker

You can bake and roast in your smoker by simply taking out the water pan and keeping your charcoal pan in the bottom position. This technique works well when cooking chicken or very thick steak. Remember that the cooking time for baking and roasting will be shorter than if you are cooking with the water. If you want to steam foods such as vegetables, don't use any wood; just let the moisture steam your veggies to perfection. Finally, you can turn your smoker into a barbecue in no time at all by removing the water pan and moving the charcoal pan up closer to the cooking grill. Then just fire it up and grill as you normally would.

Clean-up

It's important to always wait for your smoke cooker to cool before you start to clean it. First, dump out any remaining ashes once they have cooled. Then wash the water pan and the grill rack with warm soapy water. Wipe down the outside of the smoker with a damp cloth. You don't have to wash the insides of the smoker unless there is food splattered on the inside walls. Keep in mind that stain from the smoke on the inside walls is normal and does not have to be removed.

The Electric Smoker

Electric smokers are also readily available today, and some charcoal smokers can be converted to electric smokers by using an element kit. Both types of smokers will give you desired results; whether you use an electric smoker or charcoal one is just a matter of preference. As with a charcoal smoker, you can also bake, roast and steam food the same way in an electric smoker. Likewise, be sure to follow the instructions in your owner's manual.

Getting Started

The first thing to do once the smoker is assembled is to turn the control on HIGH and let it burn for 10 minutes with the lid off. This will get rid of the "new" smell, and you will only have to do this the first time that you use your new smoker. Next, spray the grid and reflector pan with cooking spray to allow for easy clean-up. Also, as you would prepare the charcoal smoker, line the water pan with heavy-duty aluminum foil. Then, place either wood chips or wood chunks so they are touching the electric coil. Fill the water pan with either hot or warm water (depending on the temperature outside). Set the control on HIGH and the cooking grid into place. You will almost always cook on HIGH unless you are just warming the food. Finally, put the hood on the smoker and let it do its magic. It's important to know that electric smoker cooking times are shorter than charcoal smoker cooking times—be sure to use a meat thermometer to check for doneness.

Clean-up

Always wait for your smoker to cool down before handling it. First, wash the cooking grid with warm soapy water to get rid of food residue. Also wash the water pan and the outside of your smoker with soapy water. If you lined the water pan with foil, clean-up will be a breeze. Lastly, wipe clean the reflector pan, element and controls. Never submerge the electrical element in water. If you clean your smoker after every use, you will get years of flavorful feasting out of it.

CHAPTER 6

FOIL COOKING

Perhaps the greatest invention for the outdoor cook since the barbecue grill is aluminum foil. It allows you to create individual pans to fit your food, and it's practical as well because it eliminates the need to wash dishes.

Foil wrap comes in two different widths, 12 and 18 inches. There are also different weights. Foil of the least weight is usually not practical for cooking items over coals, unless the food is double wrapped, because it's too easy to tear or puncture. Heavy-duty foil is excellent for making foil packages for outdoor cooking. But for really heavy jobs or when you just want to improvise your own foil pans, use extra-heavy-duty foil.

"Drugstore Wrap"

Using foil when cooking outdoors allows you to wrap food so it can be set directly on the coals. To do that you'll need to cut a piece of foil large enough to allow 4 to 6 inches of overlap on each side of your food item. Put the food in the center of the foil, then

Figure 6-1. Drugstore wrap—step 1

bring the two opposite sides together and roll down in small folds. Flatten the two remaining sides of the foil and roll in small folds toward the food. This type of packaging is called the "drugstore wrap." As with most cooking projects, using heavy-duty foil for the drugstore wrap will sufficiently seal in juices and provide trouble-free cooking.

Figure 6-2. Drugstore wrap—step 2

Figure 6-3. Completed drugstore wrap

Other Uses

You can also buy preshaped foil pans at most grocery stores. These disposable pans are excellent for cooking food items on a grill and for constructing an "oven" by clamping two of them together with a metal clamp on each side. Suspend the clamped foil pans above a few coals, then place a few more coals on top. Do not use a solid bed of briquets below the pans because it will generate too much heat. Use the foil-pan "oven" for cooking or warming food.

Foil is also useful when you want to keep food from browning too much. For example, if you are cooking a chicken on a spit and it's already golden brown, you can wrap the chicken in foil and continue roasting it until it has finished cooking. The foil will slow the browning of the food.

Insulating Foil-Cooked Food

Since foil is so thin, the heat of the charcoal briquets can easily burn food cooked in it, so keep a very close eye on it. Here's a tip: If you're cooking a hamburger patty inside foil, you can place food with a high moisture content, such as onions, lettuce, potatoes or carrots, on both sides of the patty. Since these foods contain about 90 percent water, the vegetables give off steam which will help prevent the surface of the meat from scorching.

Another convenient way of insulating the foil package itself is to wrap it in newspaper. Place the food to be cooked on the foil and use the drugstore wrap method for securing it. Then cut strips of newspaper the size of the package and wrap them around the outside of the foil package until you have a 1/8-inch-thick layer of newspaper. Vary the thickness of the paper according to the intensity of the coals and what you're cooking. Wrap the package again in foil and place above the coals. The newspapers will provide an insulating layer between the food and the coals.

Wet newspaper can also be wrapped around the first foil wrap and then placed on the coals. This method is good for foods that have a short cooking time, such as fish. The paper will be almost dry enough to flame when the food inside the foil is done. Remove the paper before it ignites. Have a spray bottle filled with water handy in case the newspaper does catch fire.

If you don't want to insulate your foil package, you can prevent burning by suspending a rack on bricks two inches above the coals. Cook your foil-wrapped food on the rack, turning at least once.

As you begin to use foil, you will find more and more uses for it in backyard cooking. Food cooked in foil can be served in it too, by brushing the ashes off the foil and turning the package seam-side-down. With a knife, cut an X from corner to corner in the foil package, peel back the foil and eat your delicious meal right out of the package.

Foil-Cooked Foods

Foil is particularly well suited to cooking vegetables. For example, butter and wrap potatoes in foil and place them in the coals before you put your steaks on to cook. You can also wrap squash, onions, peas, carrots and many other vegetables in foil and cook them with your meat or separately.

Since foil cooking uses moist heat, less-tender cuts of meat may be used as well as tender cuts.

Beef Cuts
Round steak
Flank steak
Chuck steak
Pot roast

Fish
Whole fish

Other
Turkey
Chicken
Any meats normally steamed or cooked in liquids

For some fantastic foil cooking ideas, turn to the recipe section.

CHAPTER 7

DUTCH OVEN COOKING

D utch oven cooking is one of the oldest forms of outdoor cooking, and it has remained so popular because it is easy and allows you to cook virtually any recipe whether it be by baking, roasting or frying. You can also cook using dry or moist heat depending on your needs. Dutch ovens are made from cast iron or aluminum and have thick sides, which hold heat evenly for a long period of time; a flat bottom; a close-fitting lid and a sturdy handle. Dutch ovens come in many sizes from 8 inches to 16 inches, and depending on what you are cooking, there's a size to fit your needs. There are two types of Dutch ovens, those to be used for outdoor cooking and those to be used indoors—we will explore both types of ovens.

Getting Started

The first thing you need to do when you purchase a Dutch oven is to season it. Once you have taken it out of its packaging, wash the pot and lid in hot soapy water to dissolve the protective wax residue. Then wipe it dry with a paper towel. Make sure you use a paper towel and not a cloth because a black residue will come off the oven. Since cast iron is a porous metal, you need to season it with oil so it does not rust. Heat shortening on your stove until it is completely melted, then dip a clean cloth into it and rub the oil all over the inside of the oven. Do the same around the sides, bottom and the lid of your Dutch oven. Be sure to absorb any extra oil—there should never be pools of oil remaining in the Dutch oven. The nonstick cooking surface will be built up as you continue to give your Dutch oven an oil treatment after every use.

Next, preheat your conventional oven to 350 degrees. Place the pot upside down into your oven and place the lid on top of the legs. This placement will allow any excess oil to run off, so be sure to put a cookie sheet in the bottom of your oven to catch the oil. After one hour of "baking" your Dutch oven, turn the oven off and leave the Dutch oven inside until the oven completely cools. Take the Dutch oven out and you are ready to cook.

Accessories

There are several accessories that you will find helpful as you explore the world of Dutch oven cooking:

- **Lid lifter**—this allows you to remove the lid without burning your hands; the claw end of a hammer or pliers can also be used
- **Leather gloves**—allow you to work more freely around the Dutch oven without burning your hands
- **Small brush**—to wipe the briquet ashes off the lid
- **Lid holder**—this is great to set the lid on when you are checking the food so the lid stays clean
- **Tongs**—to move the briquets around
- **Cutting board**—always helpful to have a clean surface to cut on when you are outside
- **Dutch oven table**—a metal, fireproof table on which to cook

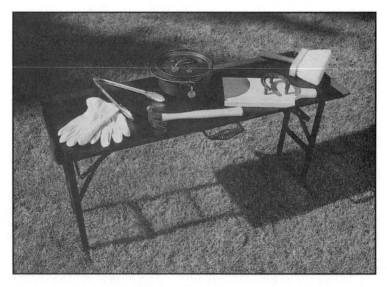

Figure 7-1. Dutch oven table and accessories

Outdoor Dutch Oven Cooking

In using your Dutch oven, you can cook up anything that you can think up—from cakes to stew. Outdoor Dutch ovens have three legs that hold the oven above the charcoal and allow air circulation under it. They also have a flat lid with a lip around the edge, which allows you to place briquets on the top of it.

Temperature Control

Most recipes that you will cook require a temperature setting of 325 degrees. There is a simple, foolproof equation for getting your oven to 325 degrees, and once you've learned it, you're on your way to becoming a master of the Dutch oven. First, pick the size of Dutch oven that you will be using. Since the 12-inch is so popular, we'll work with it (a 12-inch will hold about 6 quarts and feeds about 10 people). Take the number 12 (for the 12 inches) and subtract 3 from it, and that is how many briquets go underneath the Dutch oven. Then add 3 to the 12 and that is how many briquets go on the lid of the oven. So, for a 12-inch Dutch oven, 9 briquets go underneath and 15 briquets go on the lid to insure that your food will cook at 325 degrees. In general, two-thirds of the heat will be on top and one-third of the heat will be underneath the Dutch oven. Place the briquets so they are evenly spaced under the Dutch oven and on its lid. Also, you should always rotate your Dutch oven in order to avoid hot spots caused by the wind and briquets that may burn unevenly.

Size of Oven	# of Briquets on Lid	# of Briquets Underneath
8 inch	11	5
10 inch	13	7
12 inch	15	9
14 inch	17	11
16 inch	19	13

If you are going to be cooking several different dishes all at once, you can stack the ovens to save space and briquets. Stacking works best if you put the foods to be baked at the bottom of the stack and foods to be fried in the smaller ovens at the top of the stack. Be sure to stack the ovens with the largest at the bottom and decrease them in size as you stack. Add three briquets to the number of inches of each oven and put that many briquets on each lid. Because the ovens are on legs, enabling the air to circulate, it's okay that there will be too many briquets under each of the stacked pots.

Figure 7-2. Stacked Dutch ovens

Backyarding It with Your Dutch Oven

There are several fun places to use your Dutch oven in your own backyard.

Barbecue

You can use your charcoal barbecue as the base. Place the briquets on a foil-covered pizza pan and place it on the grilling rack. Then place the Dutch oven over the briquets. This is a great way to use your Dutch oven if you don't have any other nonflammable surface to cook on.

Figure 7-3. Dutch oven cooking on a pizza pan in a barbecue

Wheelbarrow

As you have seen in previous chapters, your wheelbarrow is a barbecuer's delight when it comes to outdoor cooking. Just fill a wheelbarrow with dirt and place bricks on top of it. Then just cook as you would in an open fire. Or, if you don't have a wheelbarrow, bricks used alone are a great surface to use because they are easily moved and allow you to create a large or small cooking surface. They will also protect the cooking area whether it be grass or your deck.

Figure 7-4. Dutch ovens cooking on bricks in a wheelbarrow

Cooking Techniques

You can cook basically anything that your heart desires in your Dutch oven. Baking, frying, roasting, boiling and spit cooking are all possible. Just spray the inside of your Dutch oven with cooking spray before you get started and clean-up will be a snap. You'll have fun experimenting with all of your favorite recipes.

Frying

Frying is a fast and easy way to prepare food in your Dutch oven. Simply put oil in the bottom of the pot and place it over the briquets. When frying, use the same number of briquets as the number of inches of the oven. For instance, if you are using a 10-inch oven, use 10 briquets underneath it; this will give you even browning of the food. You only need to put briquets under the pot when frying; you do not put the lid on the oven. To test whether the oil is hot enough to begin frying, drop flour into it—if it sizzles, you're ready to go. You can also use the lid as a frying pan by placing it upside down on either spikes or bricks. Another great idea for using the lid as a frying pan is to turn the pot upside down, put briquets on its bottom, and use the legs to prop the lid up. Frying works great for chicken and breakfast foods.

Deep-Fat Frying

Deep-fat frying is done the same way as straight frying, but you just add more oil to the bottom of the pot. Again, you do not put the lid on the Dutch oven when deep-fat frying; only put the briquets underneath. Deep-fat frying works best for fish and chips, fritters and doughnuts. The ideal temperature for deep-fat frying is 350 degrees—be sure to allow sufficient time for the oil to heat up to get desired results.

Boiling

You can use your Dutch oven to boil anything from vegetables to hot dogs. Hang the oven over an open fire from a tripod, stakes or an anchored stick. Move the briquets around so you have a rolling boil, not a fast boil, to insure that the food you are boiling does not break apart.

Stewing

Stewing is done by following the guidelines for the number of briquets underneath the oven and on its lid. First, brown the meat in the oven and then add the juices and the vegetables. With hardly any effort at all, you will soon have bubbly, delicious stew.

Roasting

When you want to cook a large piece of meat, roasting it is your best bet. Warm oil in the Dutch oven and sear all sides of the meat. Then slowly pour 1/2 to 1 cup of water over the meat, allowing it to self-baste. Season the meat and cover with the lid and briquets. Let the meat partially cook before you add your vegetables.

Baking

Most people would never dream of baking outside, but you won't believe the flavorful treats that can be baked in a Dutch oven. You can whip up cakes, pies and biscuits in the same amount of time that you could bake them in your kitchen. Baking can be done directly in the Dutch oven, or you can cook by placing a pan that is elevated with rocks in your Dutch oven. Using a pan allows air circulation and prevents your masterpiece from burning. When you are baking with sugar, be sure to line the oven with foil to make clean-up easy. You can also bake two dishes at once in one Dutch oven by lining it with foil and creating a foil divider down its middle. Two items baked at the same time should either have the same cooking time or the cooking times should be staggered.

Indoor Dutch Oven Cooking

As mentioned previously, there are Dutch ovens made specifically for the outdoors (which you know all about now) and ones made for indoor cooking in your conventional oven. An indoor Dutch oven has a flat bottom and no legs since it sits directly on the oven rack. There is also no lip on the lid, since you do not need to put briquets on it. Using a Dutch oven indoors is just as easy and convenient as outdoors, and the oven within an oven cooking technique will give you a taste that you won't believe.

If you already own an indoor Dutch oven and after reading this book you can't wait to get outdoors and try your hand at backyard survival, you can easily turn your indoor oven into an outdoor one. Just take a long piece of foil and fold the long end down 1-1/2 inches. Continue to fold until you have a 1-1/2-inch-wide collar. Join the ends together and place the foil ring on the lid of your indoor Dutch oven—now the briquets will stay put. Create legs using small metal stakes (long nails work well) or small rocks, and you're ready to cook.

Caring for Your Dutch Oven

Proper care of your Dutch oven is key to cooking delicious meals in it. Caring for your oven takes very little effort and will extend its life.

Cleaning

Keeping your Dutch oven clean is essential. If you're cooking outside, use a spatula to scrape out any food left behind. If the food is really cooked on, fill the pot with water and boil it until the food loosens. Then wipe the oven clean, dry, and use a paper towel to apply a thin coat of oil all over it.

If you are cooking inside, use warm, soapy water and a nonabrasive scrubbing pad to wash the inside of the oven. Then wipe it dry with a clean cloth or paper towel. Finally, use a paper towel to cover the entire Dutch oven with a thin coat of oil.

Storing

It's important to the flavor of your food and to the life of your Dutch oven that it be stored properly. Moisture is your Dutch oven's greatest enemy, so it is critical that it is stored in a way that no moisture will remain inside. After each use, make sure your Dutch oven is thoroughly cleaned, wiped dry and covered in a thin coat of oil. Then loosely wad up a handful of paper towels and place it inside your Dutch oven. This will absorb any moisture that may remain in the pot. Then make a collar out of aluminum foil and place it over the rim of the pot, creating a space between the pot and the lid to allow moisture to evaporate. When you store your oven for a long period of time, you may find that the oil becomes gummy. If this occurs, place the oven over glowing briquets until the residue melts and just wipe it clean with a paper towel. If your Dutch oven gets so dirty or gummy that it cannot be cleaned by hand, place it in a self-cleaning oven and all of the dirt and oil will burn off. You will need to reseason your oven if you use this method. If you care for your Dutch oven, you will get years of sumptuous meals from it. Now that your Dutch oven is cleaned and stored, it is just waiting for your next backyard adventure.

Figure 7-5.
Properly stored
Dutch oven

CHAPTER 8

STICK AND SPIT COOKING

W e've all roasted hot dogs and marshmallows over the fire; in fact, many people will tell you that's the only kind of cooking they've ever done outdoors. But to limit yourself to using sticks only to cook weenies is to cut out a major portion of fabulous outdoor cuisine. In fact, the items that can be cooked on a stick or spit, sometimes called a rotisserie, are almost limitless. By just using a little imagination, you can come up with all sorts of delicious combinations.

There are two ways of using a stick for cooking. The first is to place the food on the end of the stick, and then hold the stick over the coals and rotate it as the food cooks, or you can place kabobs on sticks and rotate them on the grill. The other, spit cooking, is used for larger items that require a longer cooking time, such as whole chicken, turkey or even a pig. The meat is placed on a large stick or metal rod that holds it above the coals while it is rotated. A rotisserie unit can be bought in most stores where you find barbecues, or you can make your own. Motorized units are available in case you don't want to keep turning the spit by hand.

Stick Cooking Basics

Stick cooking is similar to cooking on the broiler of a kitchen range. The larger the item and the deeper the heat must penetrate, the farther away from the coals the stick is held. Items placed very close to the heat will cook quickly on the outside but not on the inside. You could place a marshmallow closer to the coals, but bread dough wrapped around a stick should be placed farther away or it will burn on the outside while remaining raw on the inside.

Figure 8-1. Cooking bread on a stick

Skewers and Sticks

There are several types of commercial skewers and sticks available for outdoor cooking. Whenever you use a metal skewer, you can clean it easily by putting it back in the coals to burn off the drippings. When cool, wipe it off, and it will be ready to use again. You can also fashion a stick using a wooden dowel by sharpening one end with a pocket knife or pencil sharpener. Remember, when you use wood or bamboo skewers or sticks, soak them in water for several hours before using them so they won't burn.

Since this stick or spit method uses dry heat which does not tenderize meat, you should plan on using tender cuts of meat, ground beef balls, or less tender cuts that have been marinated and trimmed.

Figure 8-2. Apple on a stick

Beef Cuts

Filet mignon or tenderloin steak (cubed)
Spencer or rib-eye steak
Top sirloin steak (cubed)
Rib steak
Porterhouse steak (cubed)
Blade chuck steak
T-bone steak
Ground beef balls
New York steak
Liver

Pork Cuts

Pork chops (cubed)
Pork tenderloin (cubed)
Loin chops
Ham (cubed)
Link or rolled sausages
Bacon (wrapped around other pieces)

Fish and Seafood

Fillet (cubed)
Oysters
Whole fish (boned and cubed)
Large shrimp
Smoked fish

Other Meats

Chicken or turkey breasts
Wieners
Luncheon meats (cubed or wrapped
    around other pieces)
Pressed canned meat (cubed)

Kabobs

One perennial favorite in stick cooking is kabobs, which can be served as a main dish, salad, or even dessert. The nice thing about kabobs is that many different bite-sized foods can be arranged on serving plates, and everyone can take turns assembling their own favorite combinations.

If you want your kabobs to be tasty and attractive, be sure to choose foods that require about the same amount of cooking time. Combining foods that cook at different rates may result in part of the kabob burning and falling into the fire while the rest is still half-cooked. If you want to combine foods that take little cooking, such as cherry tomatoes or bananas, with foods that take longer to cook, add the faster-cooking foods at the end of the cooking time, just before you're ready to serve the kabobs. Also, avoid using small pieces of food that might pop or split when they are placed on the skewer.

Another hint for perfect kabobs is to leave a small space between the foods so they will cook more evenly and can be more thoroughly coated with sauce. If you are using foods that have fat on them, one way to prevent flare-ups is to place the charcoal briquets in rows approximately two inches apart and cook the kabobs above the space between the rows so the drippings will run into the empty area. The briquets will roast them as well as if the kabobs were suspended directly above the coals.

Spit Cooking Basics

If you're not willing to hold your food over the fire on a stick, you may want to buy or construct a spit for cooking. You'll need something to use as a crossbar to put the food on and supports to hold the bar over the coals.

Improvised Spits
Wooden dowels make convenient spits, but the wood is usually slick and smooth. In that case you should drill holes through the dowel so the food can be wired on and held steady. If you don't wire the food, it will tend to flop to the heavy side and not cook evenly. Dowels come in many different diameters so you're sure to find one that suits your needs.

Supports for Spits
You can make supports for spits in a variety of ways. One of the easiest is to use a few bricks or cement blocks, preferably the types

Figure 8-3. Chicken on a spit

that have holes in the center. Place the bricks on opposite sides of the coals where the spit is to be supported and then suspend the spit across the middle. Place two sticks vertically through two holes in each brick to keep the spit from rolling off. Again, you can control the temperature easily by removing or adding bricks. To raise the heat, remove a brick. To lower the heat, place another brick underneath, raising the food higher above the coals.

Another method of suspending the spit is to place flat rocks on top of each other to form supports above the coals. Or use two 2 x 2s, hammering nails at an angle so that a dowel spit can be suspended on the rungs formed by the nails. Place nails every two inches so the stick can be raised or lowered as the temperature

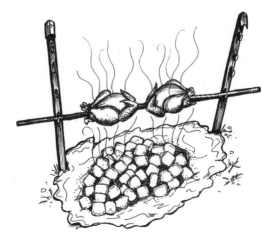

Figure 8-4. Metal pipe spit

needs to be adjusted. A similar spit can be made from two metal pipes by welding small rungs or ledges onto them so the spit can be suspended from the rungs. You should plan to weld at least two or three rungs or ledges to each pipe so the stick holding the food can be adjusted.

Meats to Cook

Like stick cooking, spit cooking uses a dry heat. You will want to use a large, tender cut of meat.

Beef Cuts—Rib roast, sirloin tip roast, top round roast

Pork Cuts—Ham or pork roast (pork requires special care to ensure it cooks thoroughly)

Other Meats—Whole chicken, Cornish game hen, game birds

Time to Cook

Prepare the food you'll be cooking on the spit, along with the marinade or sauce you're going to use for basting. Secure the food on the spit, centering it so it will cook evenly. Be sure to tie wings and legs of poultry tightly to the body so that they won't burn. Check to see that the spit is evenly balanced by suspending the loaded stick between your thumb and forefinger. If the stick rolls backward easily, it is evenly balanced.

Suspend the spit over cooking coals and begin turning. The average-sized piece of meat should cook about 8 to 10 inches away from the coals. Larger pieces will need to be farther away, and smaller pieces closer. Check the meat often so that if it is cooking too quickly, or too slowly, you can raise or lower the spit. Make sure the meat continues to rotate slowly. Food that needs to cook a long time should be rotated on a three- to five-minute basis.

You may want to baste the meat with marinade or barbecue sauce as it cooks. If you use a basting sauce that contains tomatoes or brown sugar, do not begin basting until the meat is almost cooked, because those sauces will cause the surface of the meat to burn.

CHAPTER 9

BACKYARD CAMPING

Backyard camping is not only a great getaway from everyday life, it's also terrific practice for an away-from-home camping trip. Parents and children have the chance to spend quality time together and really enjoy their backyard. Children love to camp because it is informal and they enjoy freedom from their regular routine. Parents get to escape the telephone and daily schedules. Try a backyard camping trip one night, and you'll be hooked on outdoor living.

Planning the Trip

To insure that your backyard camping excursion is a relaxing one, take the time to plan ahead. The time spent planning will not only make your "trip" more fun, it will make it less stressful—isn't that the point of camping anyway?

Family Planning Night

Planning your backyard camping trip can be just as much fun as the trip itself. Pick a night that the whole family can spend together to coordinate all of the details. Everyone should be involved, especially the children, so they feel like an important part of the trip. Why not have a mock campout in your living room on family planning night? Not only will it be fun, but it will prepare younger children for sleeping away from their bed if they never have before. Order a pizza or try a Dutch oven recipe in your conventional oven. Make popcorn. Buy a bedtime story that focuses on the outdoors—this will get everyone excited for the big trip to the backyard. Whatever you do, the planning night should be fun.

Assign one family member as the secretary. That person will take notes and keep track of all the lists you will accumulate as the family brainstorms. Make sure there is plenty of paper and pencils because details are very important. Use the lists as guides to packing everything you need for the trip. Save all of your lists from one trip to the next and create a camping file of the master lists. Also, take a pencil and a small notepad with you on the trip so you can jot down any items that you forgot. This will help you remember these items when you are packing for the next trip.

To ensure that there will be no bickering among the troops, make a duty list before you head for the backyard. Evenly assign cooking, clean-up and set-up responsibilities to all participants. You'll find that your children are much happier to wash the dishes when you're in the backyard than when you're in the house.

Choosing a Weekend

When deciding on the big date, make sure that all family members will be able to participate in the fun. Try to plan the trip during a month which generally has good weather. If your children are afraid of insects, a trip during cooler weather months might be wise because there will be fewer bugs. Planning a trip on the Saturday before a big business meeting on Monday will defeat the purpose of the trip as a stress reliever, so try to plan the night on one that is followed by a light work week. Also, the last thing you want to do is have a grumpy child who was forced to miss a big game to go on the campout.

Assigning Jobs

Everyone in the family should be assigned a job; getting all family members involved not only alleviates the pressure on Mom and Dad, it also helps the children learn responsibility. The following is a list of job assignments:

- **Meal Coordinator**—Although the whole family should help decide on the menu, this person will coordinate getting the cooking equipment and the grocery list together. When it comes time to grocery shop, this person will make sure the only purchases made are the ones on the list.

- **Equipment Coordinator**—This is an important role because without the proper equipment, the trip may be a sleepless one. This person will make sure that all of the equipment is in working order or will research what equipment to buy or rent.
- **Activities Director**—No one wants to be bored on the campout. This person will take suggestions for activities from the family and plan a schedule.
- **Mom and Dad's Helper**—Even if your children are very young, get them involved. Here's a fun idea for children who can't read a list yet. Make a collage from magazine pictures of the household items that you want them to locate and send them on a search.

Planning Meals

The most important thing to do when planning the menu for your backyard trip is to keep it simple. The trip is for fun and relaxation, not for spending hours and hours over the hot coals. First, decide on what kind of grill you are going to use. The wheelbarrow grill is the best for this kind of camping trip because it is so versatile and allows you to cook almost any desired meal. It's also great to toast marshmallows over at night. Whatever grill you decide on, plan on food that is big on nutrition, but not on bulk. Also, even though you always want your kids to eat nutritious foods, give them a little leeway and let them help plan the meals and snacks. They'll be sure to clean their plates if they get to pick what's for dinner. Here are some tips to consider when planning your menu:

- One-pot meals make preparation and clean-up a snap.
- At least one no-cook meal, such as sandwiches, makes your life easier.
- Stick cooking and foil cooking are both fun and easy. These forms of cooking let everyone prepare their own meal to their own liking.
- Sticky foods can put you in a sticky situation.
- Foods that turn soggy easily are best left in the house.

Here are some fun and delicious backyard ideas:

Chili Dog

Tie a piece of dental floss around one end of a cooked hot dog and lower it into a thermos filled with hot chili, leaving the dental floss hanging over the side. When you're ready for lunch, just pull the hot dog out of the thermos and place it on to a bun, spoon chili over it and add grated cheese. And when you're finished, you can floss your teeth!

Figure 9-1. Chili dog in a thermos and taco in a bag

Taco in a Bag

Pack individual-sized bags of corn chips and a thermos filled with hot chili. When it's time for a snack, open up the bag of chips and pour the chili over them. Use a spoon to eat your "taco." This is a no-mess, no-fuss treat.

Monster Dogs

Here's a fun way to make hot dogs a bit more fun. Cut slits in an uncooked hot dog to create arms and legs. Put it on the grill and when it begins to cook, the limbs will curl up, creating a "monster" dog.

Figure 9-2. Monster dogs

Homemade Ice Cream

Ice cream is a delicious treat for a warm day. It's also a great activity to keep the kids busy while you get a little peace and quiet. (See recipes pages 155 and 156.)

Volcano Cake

This dessert is as entertaining as it is tasty. It's a terrific way to celebrate a holiday, too. (See recipe page 152.)

Figure 9-3. Volcano cake

Dirt Dessert

Well, you can't exactly tell the kids not to play with their food when you dish up this sweet treat. This is a wonderful way to incorporate extra fun into your backyard camping trip. (See recipes pages 153 and 154 and photo on page 70.)

Figure 9-4. Dirt desserts

Equipment

The phrase "you get what you pay for" rings especially true when it comes to camping equipment. You don't want to break the bank when buying equipment, but you should spend what you can afford; your equipment should make camping easier, not turn it into a nightmare. But don't fret—you can rent equipment to see if you like camping before you buy your own gear.

Tents

A tent can make or break a camping trip. There are many different shapes and sizes available, and it's important to find the type that best suits your family's needs. Shopping at a specialty store is your best bet for finding quality equipment that will work for you. The salespeople at stores specializing in equipment for outdoor living are generally well trained and able to answer your questions.

When looking at tents, decide what size you will need depending on how many people will be sleeping in it. Remember, it's no fun being cramped on a hot summer night, so estimate larger rather than smaller. Also, if your kids are teenagers, you may want to consider buying a second tent for them. You don't want to spend the whole trip trying to get your tent pitched, so try to find one that can easily be put up and taken down. There are several things you should look for when buying a tent:

Waterproof

The tent should be colorfast and waterproof. There's nothing worse than waking up in a pool of water, and it's virtually impossible to get back to sleep once you're wet. The base of the tent should be waterproof, too, so the dew won't seep into your sleeping bag. Most tents these days are made from nylon and are both waterproof and breathable.

Strong seams

The tent should be sewn with double seams. This will help prevent the tent from ripping and also prevent water from leaking in.

Good ventilation

Your tent should allow for a breeze to blow through it and should also let light in. Also, it's good to have a tent that can be opened up to let it dry out.

Guy lines

These lines are important for the stabilization of the tent. They give the tent extra support and will prevent a rude awakening from the tent collapsing during the night.

Climate

Probably the most important consideration when buying a tent is to make sure the one that you pick is appropriate for the climate in which you will be camping.

Sleeping Bags

The type of sleeping bag you use is also a key factor in the comfort level of your trip. Sleeping bags also come in many different shapes and sizes, and every family member may not be comfortable using the same type. The kind of bag that you buy will be dependent on the climate, the season that you will be camping, your metabolism and the type of shelter you will be in; be sure you are armed with a list of questions to ask the salesperson.

The shell of a sleeping bag is made from either a synthetic fiber, such as nylon, or a natural fiber, such as cotton. The nylon will keep you dryer, but cotton breathes better.

There is a wide range of bags containing synthetic filling or down. Most sleeping bags have labels detailing the temperature range for which they are appropriate. If you are going to camp just in the spring, summer and fall, a bag with a temperature rating of +20 degrees will suffice. However, if you plan on doing winter camping, you may prefer to buy a bag with a temperature rating of 0 degrees or lower. The most important criterion to look for in a sleeping bag is one that will give you as much insulation underneath your body as on top of your body. It's impossible to stay warm through the night if you can feel the cold earth underneath you. So choose a sleeping bag in which the fiber won't compress into nothing when you lie down.

The shape of the sleeping bag is another detail to consider. Mummy bags are the warmest, but they are restricting and may not be the best choice for someone who doesn't like small spaces. A semi-mummy bag gives you a little more freedom of movement and is also very warm. A rectangular sleeping bag is not as warm because there is more space for your body to heat up, but it will prevent you from feeling claustrophobic.

Young children may not want to sleep in a sleeping bag because it is foreign to them. In that case, you can make a homemade sleeping bag using blankets. First, lay a large ground cloth out. Then layer several blankets by placing them halfway across each other. Start folding them into a tube by bringing the top blanket in from one side, the second blanket from the other side, and so on. When all of the blankets have been folded in, fold the bottom of the tube under so your child's feet won't get cold, but leave one end open so he/she can crawl into the "sleeping bag." This type of sleeping bag will be comfortable for your young ones; however, it is not waterproof. One way to keep your children dry and secure is to put their sleeping bags in an inflatable kiddie pool. The sides will make them feel protected and will keep critters out, and the rubber bottom will prevent the blankets from becoming damp.

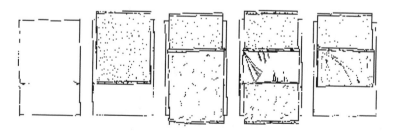

Figure 9-5. Making a homemade sleeping bag from blankets

Figure 9-6. Sleeping bag in a kiddie pool

General Camping Equipment

Many beginning campers tend to be overenthusiastic and buy every piece of camping equipment in sight. When you go shopping, bring along a friend who is a seasoned camper to help you decide on the necessities. If you're not sure whether you need a certain piece of equipment, borrow it from a friend or rent it for your first time out. Here are a few basics that you'll be glad you brought along:

Flashlight
It's nice for everyone in the family to have their own flashlight for midnight bathroom runs.

Lantern
Lanterns give off a wider ray of light than flashlights and are great if you will be playing cards or games after dark.

Mosquito Netting
This is terrific if you are really roughing it and will be sleeping out under the stars.

First Aid Kit
Hopefully you won't need it, but it's nice to have in case of an emergency.

Packing for the Trip

As you gain experience at camping, you will become accustomed to packing exactly what you need without giving it a second thought, but for now, you may need a little guidance. Just remember that although you don't want to keep on making trips to the house for items that you forgot, you also don't want all of your belongings strewn over your backyard.

How to Pack

The number of hands that will be helping to carry your supplies will determine the packing containers. If your kids are older and can help carry them, boxes work well for food and equipment. If Mom and Dad will be doing most of the manual labor, bags that can be put over the shoulder are handy to have. Backpacks are the best way to carry your tent, sleeping bag and personal items such as clothing. Even the younger children will be willing to lend a hand if they are allowed to carry their own clothes in a knapsack. Obviously, when you are camping in the backyard, the way you pack isn't that vital. However, once you start going on trips in the wilderness, you'll want all of your supplies to be as compact as possible.

Make sure you pack like items together. You don't want to have to dig through your clothes to find the can opener. This will make setting up camp a cinch and will ensure that there is a place for everything when you prepare to make the trek home.

Cooking Supplies

Once you have made up your menu, mentally walk through the preparation of each meal to determine what cooking utensils you will need. Here is a list of basic cooking supplies:

- spoons
- knives
- plates
- sharp knife
- wooden spatula
- cutting board
- grilling racks

- forks
- cups
- bowls
- metal spatula
- can opener
- heavy-duty aluminum foil
- briquets

- lighter fluid
- self-sealing plastic bags
- scrub pad
- collapsible water jug
- hot pad
- frying pan
- ice chest
- garbage bags

- matches
- dish soap and rags
- paper towels
- oven mitts
- tongs
- deep pot for boiling water
- rubber gloves

Clothes

Warm and dry—these are the key words when it comes to camping. It's very difficult to sleep when you are either cold or wet, so make the season an important factor when picking the date. When you decide on a weekend for your camping trip, it's a good idea to stick with a warm month. As you become more accustomed to camping, you may want to try your hand at winter camping, but the summer months are the easiest months in which to camp. It's always a good idea to dress in layers so you can peel off or put on clothes depending on the temperature. Again, your backyard dry run is a great way to determine your clothing necessities. You definitely don't want to overpack, but you also want to be comfortable.

Kids' Stuff

Your children may want to pack their own bags. A backyard trip is the perfect opportunity to let them pack their own clothes because you can sneak into the house later for their sweaters if you need to. Also, they will learn by experience what they need to bring. When you go on an away-from-home trip, it will be easier to explain to them why they should bring a raincoat instead of last year's Halloween costume. It's a good idea to let your child bring his/her favorite toy on the first few of outings; it will make for a more restful night's sleep all around.

The Day of the Camping Trip

Finally the big day has arrived! Hopefully you have decided on an approximate departure time so the whole family is ready at the same time. No one wants to sit around and wait while Mom runs to the grocery store one last time. Everyone should be packed and ready to go the night before.

Getting to the "Campsite"

Even if you're just traveling to your backyard, why not have a little fun getting there? Have everyone load up all of the equipment on their backs and go for a hike around the block to get to your backyard. Make believe you are hiking to get to your secluded campsite. If there is a park nearby, go for a hike around it and work your way back home. Remember, you're out to have fun!

Arriving at the Campsite

The first thing to do when you arrive at your backyard is to pick a spot to pitch the tent. Find a level spot in your yard that allows for drainage should it rain. Also, a flat area will prevent your blood from rushing to your head while you sleep as it would if you set up on an incline. Hopefully you assigned jobs on your family planning night so everyone knows what they are to do. At least two people should pitch the tent and the rest of the family should help to unload and set up camp. Once the tent(s) is set up, have everyone arrange their own personal items. If you are planning on eating soon after you arrive, the person on cooking duty should get the briquets started right away. By the time everything is set up, the briquets will be ready.

Mealtime Clean-up

Camping is a perfect way to get away from the routine of everyday life, so the last thing you want to do is spend the whole trip cleaning. Here are a few tips to make mealtime clean-up easier:
- Most importantly, keep meals simple so there aren't stacks of pots and pans to wash.
- Rinse all pots, utensils and dishes as soon as you are finished so the food will not stick.

- Boil a deep pot of water to use as your wash basin. Boiling water will sterilize the cooking equipment, but it will also be hotter than you are accustomed to so you should wear rubber gloves.
- Natural, no-rinse dish soap can be purchased; it cuts down on the amount of clean water that you need to do the dishes.
- Wash the least dirty dishes first and work your way to the dirtiest dishes. This will keep the water clean for a longer period of time.
- Have your children help out by drying the clean dishes so you don't have to set them on the ground. (The water will be too hot for them to help out with the washing.)

Activities

Camping is a good opportunity to enjoy each other's company, enjoy your backyard, and enjoy activities that you don't normally do. If the activities director asks each family member to come up with one activity, you'll be in for one fun trip.

Here are a few suggestions:

Nature Hike

The backyard is often taken for granted; your camping trip is the perfect opportunity to appreciate it. Bring along a botanical book and binoculars and learn all about the creatures and plants that you live with everyday.

Scavenger Hunt

This is as much fun for the parents to plan as it is for the kids. Make a list of items for the kids to find in the backyard. The team (or child) who finds everything on the list first gets to skip their next clean-up duty.

Nature Prints

When the scavenger hunt is over, your family can spend some quiet time making leaf prints. Simply put the leaf under a piece of paper and gently rub a pencil over the top of it. The details of the leaf will make a beautiful keepsake.

Merit Badges

Just like in Scouts, parents can set up a badge system to reward their children for helping out. Cooking, clean-up, tent-pitching, and nature skills are all badges that the children will be proud to receive. This is a great way for the kids to have fun while they're learning.

Storytelling

Whether you are toasting marshmallows over the wheelbarrow or lying around in your sleeping bags, everyone loves to hear a bedtime story. Why not invite Grandpa over to tell a story? A surprise guest is a special treat for the kids.

Stargazing

It's not often that we take the time to look at the stars above us. Bring along a book of constellations and spend some time exploring the universe.

Heading Home

All good things must come to an end and a camping trip is no different. But since your first camping trip was such a success, you'll be back in the great outdoors in no time.

Packing Up

The easiest way to break down your camp is to pack as you go along. In the morning on the final day of the trip, roll up the sleeping bags. After you use a cooking utensil for the last time, pack it in the box that you brought it in. Packing gradually lets you enjoy the last few hours of your trip because they won't be spent rushing around.

Arriving Home

Although your first instinct when you arrive home may be to jump in the shower, spend some time taking care of your equipment. Open up the tent as much as possible and let it air out. Even though it may not feel wet to the touch, any bit of moisture will cause the tent to mold and the fibers to break down. Sleeping bags and blankets need to be aired out as well so they are ready for the next trip.

Next, take a few minutes to update your master lists, adding any items that you forgot to pack and wished you had. If you wait to update your lists, you will forget what the items were and you will forget them the next trip as well. As you spend more time camping, your list will become personalized to your family's needs. Camping is a fabulous way to spend time with your family and with nature. I hope the great outdoors will become just as much a part of your life as they are of mine.

Backyard Roughing It Easy

CHAPTER 10

RECIPES

I t's been a longtime tradition among friends and families to pass along recipes. I'm happy to be able to pass some of my favorites along to you. There are so many recipes to choose from—whether it's your first time lighting up those briquets or you are a seasoned outdoor chef. There's a recipe for everyone—from the meat-lover to the veggie-lover. Some recipes can be prepared inside and then enjoyed in your backyard, while others can be easily made from scratch right under the big, open sky.

This book gives you a chance to try things you never have, experiment with new techniques—and possibly even find a new favorite recipe!

Sauces and Marinades

By creatively using sauces and marinades, you can make ordinary dishes into something new and exciting! Sauces and marinades are a staple for grilling—they add flavor to the finished dish and tenderize the meat before it is cooked. If you are looking to add something new to your summer or winter menu, make up a few of these sauces, and don't be afraid to experiment by trying them on different foods.

Here are some tips for using your sauces:

- Most of these sauces keep well for 2 to 3 weeks in the refrigerator. An easy way to store sauces is in squeeze bottles like the type usually used for ketchup and mustard. You can find bottles of this type at a kitchen or restaurant supply store.

- Many sauces work well as a marinade for meat as well as a sauce to serve over cooked foods. However, sauce that has been in contact with raw meat should NEVER be served over cooked foods unless it has been cooked along with the food. Always discard sauce that has been used as a marinade for raw meat as soon as the meat is removed from the marinade.
- See page 40 for tips on marinating.

BARBECUE SAUCE

Ingredients:
2 cups ketchup
1/2 cup soy sauce
1/2 cup dark brown sugar
1 red pepper, diced
1 onion, diced
1/4 cup Worcestershire sauce

Combine all ingredients and bring to a boil. Simmer for 20 minutes. Best if made ahead so flavors can season together. Refrigerate until ready to use. Makes about 3 cups barbecue sauce.

TERIYAKI MARINADE

Ingredients:
1/2 cup soy sauce
1/4 cup water
1/2 cup brown sugar
1-inch piece of ginger root, chopped
1 clove garlic, chopped
2 green onions, peeled and chopped
1-1/2 teaspoons sesame oil

Combine all ingredients except the sesame oil. Bring these ingredients to a boil and simmer for 10 minutes. Cool and refrigerate overnight. Strain the sauce to remove the chopped ginger root and garlic, then add the sesame oil. This sauce is good as a dipping sauce for wontons or egg rolls. It also makes an excellent marinade for meat and is good served over vegetables and rice. Makes about 1 cup marinade.

Tip: You do not have to peel the ginger root and garlic, as long as they are washed well before you chop them.

GLAZE FOR GRILLED MEATS

Ingredients:
1/2 cup ketchup
2 tablespoons light soy sauce
1/4 cup grape jelly
1/2 teaspoon granulated garlic
1 teaspoon prepared or Dijon mustard

Combine all ingredients and bring to a boil. Simmer for about 5 minutes while stirring. Makes about 3/4 cup glaze.

VINAIGRETTE DRESSING

Ingredients:
1/2 cup red wine vinegar
1 tablespoon Dijon mustard
2 tablespoons parsley, chopped
1/4 teaspoon ground black pepper
1/4 teaspoon salt
1 clove garlic, minced
1/2 cup olive oil

Mix all ingredients together except olive oil. Then, whisk in olive oil slowly. Best if made ahead so flavors can season together. This sauce is an excellent salad dressing and is also good as a marinade for poultry, fish, meat, and grilled vegetables. Makes about 1 cup vinaigrette dressing.

AVOCADO DRESSING

Ingredients:
1 avocado
juice of 1 lemon
1/2 cup olive oil
1/3 cup vinegar
salt and pepper, as desired

In food processor, blend avocado. Add lemon juice. Slowly add the olive oil and the vinegar while blending. Add salt and pepper, as desired. Makes about 1 cup dressing.

Tip: For a lite dressing, substitute low-fat yogurt for the olive oil.

SIMPLE SYRUP

Ingredients:
1 cup water
1/2 cup sugar

Boil water and sugar together until the sugar dissolves. Cool. This sauce forms a base for the fruit sauce recipes in this section. It is also good for making a moist layer cake. Simply sprinkle the cake with simple syrup or a flavored syrup (see variations below) before frosting. Makes about 1-1/2 cups syrup.

Variations: For flavored syrup, use the following ideas:
- **Orange flavor**—use a zester to remove the outside layer of the peel on an orange and add to the syrup before cooking. (A vegetable peeler may be used instead of a zester to remove the outside or orange-colored portion of the peel.)
- **Lemon flavor**—Slice 1 lemon, with the rind, and cook in the syrup.
- **Other flavors**—Use flavor extract.

PLUM SAUCE

Ingredients:
1 cup simple syrup (recipe, page 84)
4 red plums, stones removed
half of a lemon, juiced
1/8 teaspoon cinnamon (optional)

Place simple syrup in saucepan and bring to a boil. Add plums, lemon juice and cinnamon, if desired, and cook until the plums are soft. Puree the mixture. Serve over cake for a dessert, or on grilled pork chops with a pinch of pepper. Keeps for 3 weeks in the refrigerator. Makes about 2 cups sauce.

Serving idea: Marinate chicken in vinaigrette dressing (recipe, page 83) and grill. Arrange chicken pieces on plate and decorate with plum sauce.

PEACH SAUCE

Ingredients:
1 cup simple syrup (recipe, page 84)
4 fresh peaches, peeled and stones removed
2 tablespoons lemon juice

Place simple syrup in saucepan and bring to a boil. Add peaches and lemon juice and cook until the peaches are soft. Puree the mixture. Good over cake; also good as a sauce over pork loin roast. Makes about 2 cups sauce.

Variation: Mango Sauce—Follow directions for peach sauce, substituting 3 small mangoes or 1 jumbo mango for the peaches. Delicious over cake and also as a sauce over orange roughy or halibut.

GREEN WATERCRESS SAUCE

Ingredients:
2 bunches watercress
2 tablespoons lemon juice
1 clove garlic, peeled
1/2 teaspoon ground white pepper
1 cup olive oil
salt, as desired

Wash and prepare watercress, then blanch it for about 1 minute in boiling water. Remove and place in cold water for 2 minutes. When the watercress is cool, puree it together with the other ingredients, adding the olive oil gradually. If the sauce is too thick, add a small amount of warm water. Good served over green salad, fish or veal. Makes about 1-1/2 cups sauce.

ROASTED RED PEPPER SAUCE

Ingredients:
2 whole red peppers
4 tablespoons hot water
1 teaspoon chicken-flavored bouillon granules
pinch of ground black pepper
1/2 cup cream

Cut the red peppers in half and remove the seeds. Lightly toast each red pepper on the grill, or bake in oven for about 10 minutes at 300°F. Remove the skin. Dice pepper and place in blender or food processor. Add the chicken-flavored granules to the hot water and stir to dissolve. Add the broth mixture to the peppers and puree, then slowly add the cream while blending. (Be sure not to puree too long or the cream may turn to butter.) Serve over scallops, shrimp or chicken. Makes about 1 cup sauce.

Serving tip: Tastes great with mayonnaise on a grilled chicken sandwich.

LEEK SAUCE

Ingredients:
2 tablespoons butter, melted
1 cup clean, diced leeks (white part only)
2 tablespoons chopped onion
1 cup light cream
1 cup chicken broth

Sauté leeks and onion in butter until they are golden brown. Add the cream and bring to a boil. Add the chicken broth and puree. Serve over baked scallops or other seafood. Makes about 3 cups sauce.

CORN RELISH SALSA

Ingredients:
3 ears corn on the cob
3/4 cup sugar
1 cup white wine vinegar
1 jalapeno pepper with center removed, finely chopped
1/2 cup red onion, finely chopped
2 cups chopped red, yellow or green pepper
1 clove garlic, finely chopped
1 tablespoon chopped fresh cilantro
1/8 teaspoon salt
1/8 teaspoon pepper

Remove husk from corn. Place the corn on a hot grill and roast, rotating the corn with tongs as it cooks. In separate pan, cook the sugar and vinegar together until the sugar forms a string at the end of the spoon (soft ball stage). Cut the corn off the cobs. (You should have about 1-1/2 cups roasted corn.) Add corn and all other ingredients to the sugar and vinegar mixture. Bring to a boil and cook until corn is tender. Serve cold with grilled fish or other grilled meats. Makes about 4 cups.

TROPICAL FRUIT SALSA

Ingredients:
2 mangoes or papayas, diced
2 medium-sized avocados, diced
1 jalapeno pepper, diced
1/4 cup diced red onion
1/4 cup lime juice
1/3 cup lemon juice
2 tablespoons cilantro, chopped

Mix all ingredients and allow to stand for several hours in the refrigerator before serving. Good served over fish or chicken. Makes 3 cups.

GUACAMOLE

Ingredients:
2 large ripe avocados
1 to 2 teaspoons lime or lemon juice
1/2 teaspoon salt
1/8 teaspoon garlic powder
pinch of cumin
1/2 teaspoon Worcestershire sauce
1/2 cup sour cream

Peel and mash avocados. Add other ingredients and mix. Makes about 1 1/2 to 2 cups.

Appetizers

When your guests are getting hungry and your masterpiece of a main course is not ready, serve up some tasty appetizers! From fresh fruit dip to teriyaki strips, your guests will enjoy taking a bite out of their appetite.

BEAN CROSTINI

Ingredients:
1 cup small white beans, precooked
1/2 cup flavored tomato sauce
1 tablespoon fresh basil, chopped
1 baguette, sliced in rounds
fresh basil leaves
olive oil

Combine beans, tomato sauce and basil, and heat in a saucepan. Lightly toast both sides of the baguette slices under broiler. Put a spoonful of bean sauce on top of each slice. Garnish with a basil leaf. Sprinkle the finished crostini with olive oil before serving. Makes 8 to 10 crostini.

GOAT CHEESE CROSTINI

Ingredients:
1 medium baguette, sliced into circles
2 tablespoons olive oil
4 ounces goat cheese
chopped tomato (optional)
salt and pepper, as desired

Brush baguette circles with olive oil and lightly toast on both sides under the broiler. Spread each baguette circle with goat cheese and top with tomato if desired. Sprinkle with salt and pepper and broil again until cheese melts. Makes 12 crostini.

STUFFED MUSHROOMS

Ingredients:
8 to 10 large button mushrooms
salt
1/2 onion, very finely chopped
2 tablespoons olive oil
1 clove garlic, diced
1/2 cup diced green pepper
1/2 cup diced red pepper
4 slices bacon, cooked and crumbled (optional)
1 tablespoon fresh basil, finely chopped
1 cup bread crumbs

Thoroughly wash mushrooms and remove stems. Blanch mushroom caps in boiling, salted water, then cool in ice water. Place on a paper towel to drain. Finely chop the mushroom stems. Sauté the onion in olive oil. When onion browns, add chopped mushroom stems, diced garlic, red and green peppers, crumbled bacon and basil. Add bread crumbs. Stuff mushrooms and place on a grill to brown. Makes 8 to 10 stuffed mushrooms.

Note: You can make bread crumbs by cubing French bread, leaving it out to dry, then crushing the dried cubes.

GRILLED PINEAPPLE

Ingredients:
1 fresh pineapple
small amount vegetable oil

Remove the crown and rind of the pineapple. Slice pineapple and brush each piece with oil. Grill over medium heat until pineapple is warm and edges begin to caramelize. Makes 6 to 7 slices.

Variation: Place pineapple pieces on a small skewer, then brush with oil and grill.

PICKLE ROLL

Ingredients:
6 large dill pickles
6 unsliced submarine buns
1 (8-ounce) package lite cream cheese, softened

Lay pickles and rolls side by side and trim ends of rolls to make them the same length as the pickles. Then with a serrated knife, cut out the center of the roll slightly larger than the pickle. Spread cream cheese on all sides of the hole and slide in the pickle. Cut 1/2-inch slices along the roll. Makes 25 to 30 pickle roll appetizers.

Variation: Use cheese spread or seasoned cream cheese in place of the cream cheese.

PARTY ONIONS

Ingredients:
1 tablespoon milk
1 (3-ounce) package cream cheese
1 bunch (8 to 12) small green onions
1-1/2 cups shredded sharp Cheddar cheese,
    at room temperature

Thoroughly combine milk and cream cheese in a small bowl; set aside. Wash and trim onions. Spread white onion bulbs with cream cheese mixture. Roll coated bulbs in Cheddar cheese. Serves 4 to 6.

MINI-KABOBS

Ingredients:
2 boneless, skinless chicken breasts
6 to 12 button mushrooms
2 small mild onions
1 small crookneck squash, cut in pieces
1 green pepper, cut in pieces
1-1/2 cups vinaigrette dressing (recipe, page 83)
12 cherry tomatoes
6 small skewers

Cut chicken breast into small chunks. Wash and prepare the vegetables. Peel the onions, trim the ends and cut in quarters or eighths. Marinate the chicken, mushrooms, onion, pepper, and squash in vinaigrette dressing for 2 hours in the refrigerator. Skewer chicken and vegetables together and grill. (Cherry tomatoes may be added to the ends of the skewer partway through the cooking process. See tips on pages 127–129.) Serve hot as an appetizer. Serves 6.

TERIYAKI CHICKEN STRIPS

Ingredients:
10 to 12 bamboo skewers
1 pound boneless, skinless chicken breasts
1/4 cup orange juice
1/4 cup corn oil
2 tablespoons seasoned gourmet rice vinegar
1/2 teaspoon minced garlic
3 tablespoons teriyaki marinade (recipe, pages 82 and 83)
1 tablespoon fresh cilantro, chopped
1 teaspoon Hoisin sauce

Soak skewers in water. Slice chicken across the grain into strips (this is easiest to do with the chicken partially frozen). Thread the chicken strips onto the skewers and place in a dish. Meanwhile, mix all the other ingredients to make a marinade for the chicken. Pour this sauce over the chicken and allow to marinate for at least 1 hour in refrigerator. Discard leftover marinade. Cook on a grill or over coals. Serves 4 to 6.

Variation: Use flank steak, London broil or turkey breast in the place of the chicken. (See figure 1-19 on page 9—teriyaki strips on flowerpot grill.)

TERIYAKI ROLL-UPS

Ingredients:
1 pound top round steak or London broil
1/2 pound center cut or lean bacon
1 cup teriyaki marinade (recipe, pages 82 and 83)
toothpicks

Thinly slice meat across the grain, about 1/8 inch thick. (Ask a butcher to do this for you when you purchase the meat, or partially freeze the meat, then slice.) Lay out strips of bacon, stretching them as long as they will go. Place strips of meat on the bacon and roll. Secure with toothpicks. Marinate meat rolls in teriyaki marinade for 4 to 6 hours in the refrigerator. Discard leftover marinade. Grill until steak and bacon are done. Serves 4 to 6.

Variation: May also be used as a main course served with other oriental foods.

FRESH FRUIT DIP

Ingredients:
1 (3-ounce) package lite cream cheese (softened)
1/4 can frozen lemonade concentrate
2 to 3 tablespoons sugar
1/2 cup plain yogurt
1/2 cup whipped topping

Blend cream cheese, lemonade concentrate and sugar. Add yogurt. Fold in whipped topping and chill. Serve with pieces of fruit or melon. Makes 1-1/4 cups fruit dip.

Beverages

Summer or winter, indoors or out, hot ones or cold ones—
creative drinks are perfect for any occasion!

ISLAND PUNCH

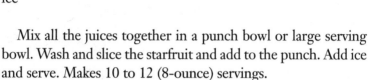

Ingredients:
1 (1 pint) can of each of the following fruit juices:
- passion fruit
- mango
- papaya
- pineapple
- orange
- cranberry (optional)

1 star fruit
ice

Mix all the juices together in a punch bowl or large serving
bowl. Wash and slice the starfruit and add to the punch. Add ice
and serve. Makes 10 to 12 (8-ounce) servings.

Tip: See pages 27 and 34 for more serving ideas!

CRANBERRY ICE

Ingredients:
1 (12-ounce) package fresh or frozen cranberries
2 cups sugar
4 cups water
juice of 3 lemons
1 teaspoon grated orange peel

Boil cranberries, sugar and 2 cups water together until
berries pop. Process in a blender until smooth. Add lemon
juice, 2 cups water and orange peel. Freeze in a plastic container. Remove from freezer about 1 hour before serving. Slush
with a fork or in the blender. Serves 4 to 6.

Variation: Add chilled lemon-lime soda to slush, if desired.

HOT CIDER

Ingredients:
2 quarts apple cider
1/4 cup brown sugar
1/3 cup honey
8 cinnamon sticks
3 fresh apples, finely diced
extra cinnamon sticks for garnish (optional)

Simmer cider, sugar and honey together, stirring until sugar and honey dissolve. Add cinnamon sticks and diced apples and simmer together for an additional 1 to 2 hours. Serve hot in glass mug with cinnamon stick in each one. Makes 2-1/2 quarts of spiced cider.

ORANGE SUPREME FLOAT

Ingredients:
12 large oranges
1 pint orange sherbet
1 (1-liter) bottle orange soda

Cut the top quarter off each orange. With a grapefruit or paring knife, cut around the inside of the orange as you would a grapefruit. Spoon out and remove all the orange pulp, place it in a container and store pulp in the refrigerator to use for breakfast juice. When ready to serve, nestle a small scoop of orange sherbet into an orange shell, then pour orange soda over the top. Serve with a straw. You will be amazed how the flavors blend to create a novel dessert. Serves 12.

FRUIT PUNCH

Ingredients:
1 package (makes 2 quarts) unsweetened orange-flavored
    drink mix
1 package (makes 2 quarts) unsweetened cherry-flavored
    drink mix

1 (6-ounce) can frozen orange juice concentrate, thawed
2 cups sugar
1-1/2 cups pineapple juice
2 bananas, mashed
water
1 (1-liter) bottle lemon-lime soda

Mix drink mixes, orange juice, sugar, pineapple juice and bananas together thoroughly. Add enough cold water to make 1 gallon of juice. This mixture can be frozen to be used at a later date, or stored in the refrigerator. Just before serving, add chilled lemon-lime soda to punch. Serves 16 to 20.

DAFFODIL FRAPPE PUNCH

Ingredients:
6 cups water
3 cups sugar
1 (3-ounce) package lemon gelatin
juice of 3 lemons
juice of 3 oranges
1-1/2 cups pineapple juice
3 bananas, blended
1 (2-liter) bottle ginger ale
12 daffodils, for garnish

Heat water and sugar together until sugar dissolves. Add gelatin and stir until dissolved, then cool. When cool, add lemon, orange and pineapple juices. Freeze in ice cube trays. (Frozen drink cubes may be removed from the trays and stored in a zip-top bag after they are frozen.) One hour before serving, remove drink cubes from freezer and place in a drink pitcher to thaw. Just before serving, stir the blended bananas into the slushy juice. Fill tumblers half-full with the fruit drink mixture, then fill to the top with ginger ale and stir. Cut daffodil stems so that each stem is no more than 2 to 3 inches long. Wash the stems. Slip a daffodil stem into each straw so flower head stands up. Serve with daffodil-straw sticking up from drink in tumbler. Serves 12.

TOMATO SEAFOOD COCKTAIL

Ingredients:

1 quart tomato juice
1 (12-ounce) bottle seafood cocktail sauce
1 tablespoon Worcestershire sauce
1/2 cup lemon juice
1-1/2 tablespoons white vinegar
1 tablespoon mild horseradish
2 tablespoons sugar
1/4 teaspoon garlic salt
1 diced green onion (optional)
2 cups diced celery
1/4 to 1/2 pound fresh cooked tiny shrimp or crab
8 large shrimp for garnish

Mix all of the above ingredients. Chill for 24 hours. Serve either hot or cold in clear glasses with a shrimp over the side. To be eaten with a spoon. Serves 8 to 10.

Grill Cooking

Gas grill, flowerpot grill, wheelbarrow grill—whether you have a big backyard or just a balcony, you can grill! Now that you've read all about grills and grilling (chapter 4), it's time to cook up some recipes that will make you wonder if you'll ever want to go back inside again.

CLAM BAKE ON GRILL

Ingredients:
fresh seaweed (optional)
1 lobster (1 to 1-1/4 pounds)
4 littleneck clams
1 small Polish or chorizo sausage, grilled and cut in half
2 small red potatoes, partially cooked
1 cob of corn, shucked and broken in half
1 small red onion, sliced
2 plum tomatoes, cut in wedges
1/2 lemon, cut in wedges
parsley sprigs
2 sheets heavy-duty aluminum foil, 18 by 24 inches

On one sheet of foil place a layer of seaweed. Place the lobster on top of the seaweed and arrange all the other ingredients around the lobster. Close the foil using the drugstore-wrap method (see pages 47 and 48). Wrap the package again to prevent it from leaking during the cooking process. Place the clam bake package on a hot grill and cook for 15 to 20 minutes. Serves 2.

GRILLED ARCTIC SHAR

Ingredients:
1 (10- to 12-ounce) fillet Arctic Shar
vinaigrette dressing (recipe, page 83)
oil

Debone fillet by running your finger from the head of the fish to the tail; when you feel a bone, pull it out. Preheat the grill and oil the rack. Brush both sides of the fish with vinaigrette dressing. Place the fish, flesh side down, on the hot rack. Cook until the skin begins to puff and the edge of the skin begins to brown. Loosen the fish with a spatula, then turn and brush again with vinaigrette dressing. Cook on the skin side until fish is done (flesh in the middle of the fish flakes easily with a fork). Serves 2.

SALMON ON THE GRILL

Ingredients:
2 (6- to 8-ounce) salmon fillets
vinaigrette dressing (recipe, page 83)
oil

Preheat the grill. Brush both sides of the fillets with vinaigrette dressing. Lightly oil the hot grill rack and place the fish on it. Cook until the meat begins to brown around the edges. Use a spatula to loosen the fish underneath, then turn and brush again with vinaigrette dressing. Cook on the other side until the fish is done (flesh in the middle of the fish flakes easily with a fork). Serves 2.

TERIYAKI CHICKEN

Ingredients:
3 pounds chicken breasts and thighs
2 cups teriyaki marinade (recipe, pages 82 and 83)

Boil chicken pieces in a large pot of water for about 20 minutes or until almost cooked. (Skin may be removed from the pieces either before or after boiling.) Place the chicken pieces in 1 cup of the premade teriyaki sauce and marinate overnight in the refrigerator. Discard marinade and arrange meat on a grill to barbecue. Serve with rice. Spoon fresh teriyaki sauce over the rice. Serves 6.

Variation: Use 3 boneless, skinless chicken breasts and cook as above. Slice the meat in strips and serve on buns with mayonnaise, Dijon mustard, sliced tomatoes and sliced onion, as desired.

GRILLED STEAKS

Ingredients:
2 beef steaks (see pages 38 and 39 for tips on the best cuts
    for grilling)
salt
pepper
2 tablespoons vegetable oil

Sprinkle steaks with salt and pepper. Oil the grill and brush the steaks lightly with oil. Place steaks on hot grill and cook to desired doneness. Serves 2.

Tip: A quick and easy way to test for doneness is described on page 40.

GRILLED BEEF BURRITO

Equipment:
small-holed grilling sheet (see pages 37 and 38) or
    foil pan with holes punched in it
nonstick cooking spray

Ingredients:
2 to 3 tomatoes, diced
5 green onions, chopped
1/4 cup chopped cilantro
1/4 teaspoon garlic salt
1 (2 to 3 pound) sirloin tip roast, uncooked, diced
6 to 8 large flour tortillas
2 to 3 avocados, mashed (add 1 teaspoon lemon juice)
    or sliced
hot sauce or salsa (optional)

Combine the tomatoes, green onions, cilantro and garlic salt in a bowl and set aside. Preheat the small-holed grilling sheet on the grill. Spray it with nonstick spray and begin cooking the meat. When the meat is done, warm the tortillas. This may be done by removing the small-holed grilling sheet and placing each tortilla on the grill for about half a minute. Fill each tortilla with a small amount of meat. Top the meat with 2 or 3 avocado slices or about 2 tablespoons mashed avocado. Sprinkle with about 1 to 2 tablespoons of the tomato mixture. Fold in the ends of the tortilla and roll. Serve hot with hot sauce or salsa as desired. Makes 6 to 8 burritos.

GRILLED BABY BACK RIBS

Ingredients:
2 pounds pork baby back ribs
2 cups barbecue sauce (recipe, page 82)
2 tablespoons oil

Place ribs in a large kettle. Cover with cold water, then bring to a boil. Turn down heat and simmer slowly until the ribs are tender, about 40 minutes. Drain water off the ribs and place in a covered container in the refrigerator until ready to grill. When ready to grill, cut the ribs into 3- to 4-rib servings. Brush the ribs with oil and place on the grill. When ribs are heated through, brush them with barbecue sauce on both sides and continue to heat until the sauce begins to caramelize. Serve ribs with extra barbecue sauce. Serves 2 to 3.

GRILLED PORK CHOPS

Ingredients:
1 cup vinaigrette dressing (recipe, page 83)
4 pork chops
fresh rosemary or thyme, for garnish

Divide vinaigrette dressing in half. Marinate chops in half the vinaigrette dressing overnight in the refrigerator. Discard marinade and grill the chops 10 to 15 minutes per side on a hot grill. Before serving brush meat with vinaigrette dressing not previously used for marinating. Garnish with fresh rosemary or thyme. Serves 4.

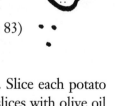

GRILLED POTATOES

Ingredients:
4 large red potatoes
olive oil or vinaigrette dressing (recipe, page 83)
seasoned salt (optional)

Boil the potatoes until soft, but still firm. Slice each potato into 1/2-inch-thick round slices. Brush the slices with olive oil or vinaigrette and sprinkle with seasoned salt as desired. Place on a hot grill. When potatoes start to brown lightly, turn and grill the other side. Serves 4 to 6.

GRILLED PORTABELLA MUSHROOMS

Ingredients:

2 Portabella mushrooms, sliced

1/2 cup low-fat Italian or vinaigrette dressing (recipe, page 83)

Coat mushroom slices on all sides with dressing. If desired, slices may be marinated in the dressing for a few minutes to 1 hour. Place mushroom slices on a hot grill. Grill until the mushrooms become soft, turning once while cooking. (See photo, page 37.) Serve as a side dish or appetizer. Makes about 8 mushroom slices.

GRILLED VEGETABLES

Equipment:

small-holed grilling rack (see pages 37 and 38)

Ingredients:

1 medium zucchini, cut into 1/2-inch slices

1 medium crookneck squash, cut into 1/2-inch slices

1 yellow pepper, seeded and cut into quarters

1 red pepper, seeded and cut into quarters

1 green pepper, seeded and cut into quarters

4 to 5 button mushrooms, cut in half or sliced

1 red onion, sliced

1 bunch green onions, trimmed to a length of about
    4 inches (optional)

1 sweet potato, precooked and cut into 1/2-inch slices
    (optional)

1/2 to 1 cup vinaigrette dressing (recipe, page 83)

1 tablespoon oil

Marinate the prepared vegetables in vinaigrette dressing for 1 to 2 hours. Place vegetable pieces on a small-holed grilling rack on a hot grill. Brush with vinaigrette dressing while grilling. Serves 6 to 8.

GRILLED VEGETABLE SANDWICH

Ingredients:
1 medium eggplant
2 small zucchini
2 yellow squash
1 onion
1 red pepper
olive oil
1 fresh tomato
4 foccacia breads
4 ounces goat cheese or mozzarella cheese (optional)
avocado dressing (optional) (recipe, page 84)

Slice eggplant, zucchini, yellow squash and onion in 1/4-inch slices. Divide pepper in quarters, clean seeds out and flatten each section by pressing it with the palm of your hand. Brush these vegetables with olive oil and cook on a grill. Slice the tomatoes. With a sharp knife slice around the edge of the bread so the top separates from the bottom. Lay vegetables evenly on the base of the bread. Layer cheese and tomato slices over the vegetables. Spread with avocado dressing, if desired, and replace the top of the bread. Serves 4.

Note: Foccacia is a type of Italian bread. It is flat and round or oval—perfect for this kind of sandwich.

Smoke Cooking

Ah, the smell of hickory in the air . . . someone must be smoke cooking. Why not delight your family's palate with one of these tasty recipes. Smoke cooking may take a little longer than grilling, but it requires minimal maintenance once you get started and the results are fabulous.

SMOKED SALMON

Ingredients:
2 teaspoons fresh, minced dill
1 teaspoon ground black pepper
2 teaspoons course salt
2 teaspoons dried coriander
2 (6- to 10-ounce) boneless, skinless salmon fillets

Mix all spices together and rub on all surfaces of the salmon fillets. Place in preheated smoker. Smoke for 1/2 hour per pound of salmon.

SMOKED TURKEY

Ingredients:
1 (9- to 12-pound) whole turkey
8 to 10 fresh sage leaves
1 tablespoon coarse salt
2 teaspoons paprika (Hungarian)
2 teaspoons garlic powder
1 teaspoon onion powder
dash of cayenne pepper
1/4 cup vegetable oil

Remove turkey giblets and wash and pat the turkey dry. Place 4 to 5 sage leaves under the breast skin on each side of the turkey. Combine salt, spices and oil and mix well. Gently rub the mixture into the skin of the turkey—paying special attention to the legs and wings. Allow to stand at room temperature for 30 minutes. Preheat smoker using hickory or fruitwood. Smoke turkey allowing 1-1/4 hours per pound until a meat thermometer (inserted into the thickest part of the thigh) registers 185°F. To speed up the smoking process, pre-cook the turkey in the oven for 2 hours and then place it immediately into the smoker.

SMOKED HERBAL PORK

Ingredients:
2 teaspoons dried oregano
2 teaspoons dried basil
2 teaspoons dried thyme
1 teaspoon garlic powder
1 teaspoon onion powder
1 tablespoon course salt
1 (3- to 5-pound) pork picnic roast
aluminum foil

Combine all spices and rub over the entire roast. Place in preheated smoker using hickory or fruit wood. Allow to smoke for 1 to 1-1/4 hours per pound of meat or until meat thermometer registers 170°F. Loosely cover in foil and let stand for 15 minutes before carving.

Foil Cooking

Foil cooking is easy and versatile and allows for quick clean-up. Aluminum foil enables you to cook food to perfection, whether you're cooking on open coals or cooking on your gas grill. For tips on successful foil cooking, read chapter 6.

CORNISH HEN IN A BACKPACK

Equipment:
3 medium-sized (fist-sized) rocks
18-inch heavy-duty aluminum foil
2-inch stack of newspapers
small backpack

Ingredients:
1 Cornish hen
1/2 cup barbecue sauce

Select smooth rocks that do not have splits or cracks. (Sandstone, limestone and rocks that contain moisture should not be used.) Heat the rocks in a hot fire for 30 to 45 minutes. Meanwhile, unfold and lay out a stack of newspapers about 1/2 inch thick. Place a sheet of heavy-duty foil (about 18 by 24 inches) on the newspaper. Wash the Cornish hen and center it on the foil. Using tongs, carefully remove the rocks from the fire and wrap them in foil. (Be sure to wear gloves or oven mitts while handling the hot rocks.) Place one medium-sized rock in the cavity of the Cornish hen and place a rock on each side of the breast. Pour barbecue sauce over the Cornish hen, then bring the foil up and fold it together using the drugstore-wrap method (see pages 47 and 48). Pull the foil package to one corner of the newspaper and begin to roll the bird, folding in the sides of the newspaper as you go. Continue wrapping in newspaper until you have a large, thick bundle. Place the bundle in a backpack and go for a hike, or, if you are staying in your backyard, just place the bundle in a cardboard box. The heat from the rocks will cook the chicken while you hike or play. In about 1-1/2 hours the Cornish hen will be ready to eat. Serves 2.

Note: This same procedure works for chicken. Select rocks slightly larger than those described above. Follow all other steps as outlined, but allow the chicken 2 to 2-1/2 hours to cook.

Variation: When cooking a Cornish hen in a backpack or box, you can cook a whole meal at once! Here's how: just arrange 2 to 3 small red potatoes and a cob of corn broken in half around the Cornish hen in the foil pack. Close the pack and cook as outlined above. (This variation should be used only with Cornish hen, not with chicken.)

FOIL DINNER

Ingredients:
2 large onions, sliced
1 pound lean ground beef, formed into 4 patties
4 teaspoons dry gravy mix
1/2 teaspoon seasoned salt
1/4 teaspoon ground black pepper
3 to 4 carrots, thinly sliced
3 to 4 potatoes, thinly sliced
4 pieces heavy-duty aluminum foil, 14 by 18 inches

Place 1 to 2 slices of onion and 1 hamburger patty in the center of a square of foil. Sprinkle the meat with 1 teaspoon gravy mix and seasoned salt and pepper, as desired. Place carrots and potatoes over the meat and top with 1 more slice of onion (if desired). Seal the foil using the drugstore-wrap method (see pages 47 and 48). Place the pack on hot coals and cook for 10 to 15 minutes per side. Check for doneness of meat and cook longer as needed. Serves 4.

MEAT LOAF IN AN ONION

Ingredients:

1 pound lean ground beef
1 egg
1/4 cup cracker crumbs
1/4 cup tomato sauce
1/8 teaspoon pepper
1/2 teaspoon salt
1/2 teaspoon dry mustard
6 large onions, peeled and halved
6 pieces heavy-duty aluminum foil, 14 by 18 inches

In a medium bowl, mix ground beef, egg, cracker crumbs, tomato sauce, pepper, salt and dry mustard. Set aside. Cut onions in half horizontally and remove center part of onion, leaving 3/4-inch shell. Divide meat mixture into 6 portions and roll into balls. Place in the centers of the onions and put onion halves back together. Wrap each onion in foil using the drug-store-wrap method (see pages 47 and 48). Cook on coals for 15 or 20 minutes per side, depending on the size of the onion. Serves 6.

Variation: For a simple and quick version of this recipe, omit the egg, cracker crumbs, tomato sauce and dry mustard. Mix the meat and salt and pepper and place in onions as described above.

INSIDE-OUT HAMBURGER

Ingredients:

2 pounds lean ground beef
2 large onions, sliced
1 or more fillings (see list below)
salt and pepper, as desired
6 to 7 pieces heavy-duty aluminum foil, 12 by 18 inches

Divide ground beef into 12 or 14 equal portions. Form into balls and roll out into large, thin, round patties. Place two slices of onion on a piece of foil and top with beef patty. In the center of the patty place one or more of the fillings listed below or any other filling that goes well with meat. Leave about 1/2-inch space around the edge of the patty. Place another meat patty over the fillings and gently seal the two patties together around the edges. Sprinkle with salt and pepper, as desired. Place two more onion slices on top and close the foil around the inside-out hamburger using the drugstore-wrap method (see pages 47 and 48). Repeat these steps until all the patties are used. Cook for 12 minutes per side on hot coals. Serves 6 to 7.

Fillings:

- grated Cheddar cheese
- barbecue sauce
- sliced mushrooms
- fresh parsley
- cooked bacon
- chopped onion
- pickles
- chopped tomato
- crumbled bleu cheese
- chili
- chopped green pepper
- relish
- salsa
- zucchini

SAUSAGE-SAUERKRAUT SPLIT

Ingredients:
8 polish sausages
1/2 pound block Swiss cheese
1 (16-ounce) can sauerkraut
4 pieces heavy-duty aluminum foil, 14 by 18 inches

Split sausages down the center. Cut cheese in wedges and place in splits. Divide the sauerkraut into four equal portions and place one portion in the center of each piece of foil. Place two sausages on each portion of sauerkraut and spoon some of the sauerkraut over the sausages. Seal foil, using the drugstore-wrap method (see pages 47 and 48). Cook on a wire rack 2 inches above the coals. Cook 10 minutes on each side. Yields 4 (2 sausage) servings.

TROUT IN FOIL

Ingredients:
1 trout
1 tablespoon butter
salt and pepper, as desired
1/2 lemon, sliced
lemon juice (optional)
1 piece of heavy-duty aluminum foil, 12 by 18 inches

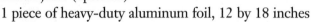

Remove fins and head of the fish. Rub with butter, salt and pepper. Place on sheet of foil and lay lemon slices along the length of the fish. Seal the package using the drugstore-wrap method (see pages 47 and 48). Place on wire grill 2 to 3 inches above glowing coals or charcoal, or insulate the foil package and place directly on the coals (see page 49). Cook about 10 to 15 minutes on each side. Serve with lemon juice, if desired. Serves 1.

Deboning a Trout: After trout has been cooked in foil, take a knife and cut along the backbone of the fish. Carefully lift both sides of the fish away from the bone at the tail end. Firmly hold the tail and lift it up carefully, letting the meat drop away from the bone. If the trout is well cooked, the fish will come clean of the bones. This method of deboning will work with any freshwater fish.

Note: You can use this same cooking method with fish fillets. Rub the fillet with butter, salt and pepper; wrap with lemons; and cook as described above. Try substituting chopped onion for the lemon slices.

BUTTERNUT SQUASH

Ingredients:
1 butternut squash
2 tablespoons butter
1 tablespoon brown sugar
salt and pepper
2 pieces heavy-duty aluminum foil, 14 by 18 inches

Cut squash in half; scoop out seeds. Place butter and brown sugar in each half and sprinkle with salt and pepper. Wrap each half in heavy-duty foil, using the drugstore-wrap method (see pages 47 and 48). Place on wire grill 2 to 3 inches above glowing coals, or insulate the package with newspaper (see page 49), and cook directly on the coals. Cook for 10 to 15 minutes on each side. Cook the cut-side up first so the butter cooks into the squash. Serves 2.

FRESH CORN ON THE COB

Ingredients:
corn on the cob
water
butter and seasoning, as desired
aluminum foil (optional)

Select tender, juicy ears of corn. Peel back the husks from the corn about 1 inch and remove the top silk. Pull husks back over the corn and soak in water for 1 hour. Place on coals in the husk or wrap in foil and place on coals. Cook for about 5 minutes per side. Unwrap, pull husk back, and add butter and seasoning as desired.

CHINESE VEG PACK

Ingredients:
1 stalk celery, thinly sliced on an angle
1 green pepper, cut in strips
6 large button mushrooms, cut in half
1 medium onion, thinly sliced
1 piece of heavy-duty aluminum foil, 15 by 18 inches
2 to 3 tablespoons teriyaki marinade (recipe, pages 82 and 83)
ground black pepper (optional)

Place celery, green pepper, mushrooms and onion on the foil. Sprinkle with teriyaki marinade and pepper if desired. Seal the foil using the drugstore-wrap method (see pages 47 and 48). Cook on grill for 15 minutes per side. Serves 3 to 4.

BANANA BOATS

Ingredients:
4 bananas, in the peel
1/2 cup milk-chocolate pieces
1/2 cup miniature marshmallows
heavy-duty foil

Cut a slit along the length of each banana. Fill the slit with milk-chocolate pieces and marshmallows and wrap securely in heavy-duty foil. Heat for about 5 minutes over coals until chocolate and marshmallows melt. Serves 4.

Tip: For an indoor treat, leave off the foil and warm banana boats in the microwave until marshmallows melt.

Variation—Hawaiian Banana Boats: Prepare the bananas as above but fill slit with pineapple chunks, brown sugar and coconut.

BAKED APPLE BAR

Ingredients:

1 cooking apple per person
1 or more of the fillings listed below
1 (12-by-14-inch) piece heavy-duty aluminum foil per apple

Core each apple, taking care to remove the core, but not cut all the way through the apple. Make the cavity large enough so that a filling can be placed into it. Fill with 1 or more of the filling ingredients listed below. Place the apple on a piece of foil. Bring the foil to the top, twist it around and place on a wire grill 2 to 3 inches above the glowing coals. Cook for 30 to 45 minutes, keeping the apple open-end up. To serve, open the foil up like a bowl and eat with a spoon. Serve with cream or vanilla ice cream. Serves 1.

Fillings:

- brown sugar
- nuts
- raisins
- dried cherries
- butterscotch chips

- red hots
- cinnamon sugar
- dried cranberries
- dates
- butter

ORANGE CUPCAKES

Ingredients:

1 orange per person
1 (18-1/2-ounce) package yellow or spice cake mix, prepared
    according to package directions, but not baked
1 (12-inch) square piece of heavy-duty foil per orange

Cut 1-inch slice from top of each orange. Scoop out orange fruit and pulp. Leave peel intact as a baking cup. Fill each orange peel 2/3 full with prepared cake batter. Replace top of each orange. Place a filled orange in center of each piece of foil. Bring foil together at the top and twist tight. Place wrapped oranges in coals for 15 to 20 minutes to bake. One cake mix will fill 12 to 18 oranges.

APPLE BREAD PUDDING

Ingredients:
1/4 loaf French bread
2 tablespoons butter
2 tart apples
juice of 1 lemon
1/4 cup brown sugar
1/2 teaspoon cinnamon
1/4 cup raisins
1/4 cup apple cider
1/2 cup chopped nuts (walnuts or mixed nuts)
2 pieces heavy-duty aluminum foil, 12 by 18 inches

Cut bread lengthwise in 1/2-inch slices. Butter both sides and cut into 1-inch cubes. Place in a large mixing bowl. Core and cut apples into small cubes and add to the bread. Add the lemon juice, sugar, cinnamon, raisins, apple cider, and nuts. Mix. Divide mixture in half and place each portion on a piece of foil and wrap using the drugstore-wrap method (see pages 47 and 48). Place on wire rack 2 to 3 inches above the glowing coals or double wrap with foil, newspapers and foil (see page 49) and place directly on coals. Cook for 20 minutes per side. Unwrap and top with ice cream. Serve immediately. Serves 4 to 6.

Dutch Oven Cooking

As one of the oldest forms of outdoor cooking, Dutch oven cooking is one of my favorite ways to prepare a meal. Roasting, stewing, frying—even baking—anything is possible in a Dutch oven. Once you have mastered the skill of Dutch oven cooking (see chapter 7), you will never want to use your conventional oven again.

PIZZELLE CRUST

Ingredients:

1/2 cup warm water
1 tablespoon active dry yeast
1-1/2 teaspoons sugar
2/3 cup warm water
4 cups bread flour or all-purpose flour
1-1/2 teaspoons olive oil
1 teaspoon salt
extra olive oil

Place 1/2 cup warm water in a mixing bowl and sprinkle the yeast and sugar over the top. Stir well and allow to stand 8 to 10 minutes. Add the flour, 1-1/2 teaspoons olive oil and salt and begin to mix using a dough hook or food processor. Gradually add the remaining water. When a smooth dough forms, continue to beat or knead the dough for an additional 10 to 15 minutes. Transfer the dough to a lightly-oiled bowl, turning the dough once in the bowl so that the top of the dough becomes lightly coated with oil. Cover the dough loosely with plastic wrap and let it stand in a warm place until double in volume. Punch down the dough and portion off the amount of dough needed to make a thin crust the size of the pan being used (about half). Stretch the dough out thin and place it in the pizza pan. Brush the dough with olive oil, add toppings and bake for about 30 minutes at 325°F in oven or Dutch oven. Remaining dough may be kept in the refrigerator until ready to be used. Makes 2 thin 10-inch pizzelle crusts.

GOAT CHEESE AND CARAMELIZED ONION PIZZELLE

Equipment:
frying pan (optional)
12- or 14-inch Dutch oven
10- or 12-inch round pizza pan, slightly smaller than the
   Dutch oven
small stones or 3 jar rings for elevating the pizza pan

Ingredients:
1 pizzelle crust (recipe, page 117)
olive oil
2 medium onions, sliced
salt
pepper
2 tomatoes, thinly sliced (optional)
8 ounces goat cheese, sliced

Prepare pizzelle crust and brush it with olive oil. Sauté the onions in olive oil in a frying pan or Dutch oven until they are browned and caramelized. Sprinkle with salt and pepper, as desired. Drain any moisture from the onions and spread them on the crust. Top with the tomatoes and goat cheese. Bake on a round pizza pan inside the Dutch oven at 325°F. Bake until crust is cooked and cheese is melted, about 30 minutes. Serves 4.

DEEP-DISH PIZZA CRUST

Ingredients:
1-1/4 cups warm water
2 teaspoons sugar
4 teaspoons active dry yeast
2 teaspoons oil
scant 1/2 teaspoon salt
4 cups all-purpose flour
extra oil

Place water in a mixing bowl. Sprinkle the sugar and yeast over the top and stir until dissolved. Place bowl in a warm place and allow to stand until yeast begins to bubble (about 8 to 10 minutes). Add the 2 teaspoons of oil, the salt and 3-1/2 cups of flour. Mix using a dough hook or food processor. Knead the dough for about 15 minutes or until the dough takes on a smooth texture, adding more flour as needed. Transfer the dough to a lightly-oiled bowl, turning the dough once in the bowl so that the top of the dough becomes lightly coated with oil. Cover the bowl loosely with plastic wrap and let stand in a warm place until double in volume. Punch down the dough and press it out evenly in the bottom of a lightly oiled 12-inch Dutch oven. Brush crust, especially edges, with oil. Bake in Dutch oven at 325°F for 15 to 20 minutes. Remove lid, add toppings and bake for an additional 20 to 30 minutes. Makes enough dough for 1 large (12- to 14-inch) deep-dish pizza.

GOURMET VEGETABLE DEEP-PAN PIZZA

Ingredients:
1 deep-dish pizza crust (see recipe, page 118)
oil
1/4 to 1/2 cup low-fat ranch or
    Parmesan Italian salad dressing
3 cups grated or shredded mozzarella cheese
1 cup fresh leaf spinach, washed, trimmed and shredded
1 sliced zucchini
1 chopped tomato
1/4 cup chopped purple onion
1/4 cup chopped green onion
1 (6-ounce) bottle marinated artichoke hearts, drained

Prepare pizza crust dough. Lightly coat the Dutch oven with oil. Spread the dough in the bottom of the pan and brush lightly with oil. Place the lid on the Dutch oven and bake at 325°F for 15 to 20 minutes. Remove the lid and spread the crust with the salad dressing and half of the cheese. Cover the cheese with a single layer of spinach leaves, then add in layers the zucchini, tomatoes, onions and artichoke hearts. Top the pizza with the rest of the cheese. Bake for an additional 20 to 30 minutes or until the cheese is melted and bubbly. Serves 4 to 6.

Variation: Rather than baking the crust then adding the toppings, you can put the toppings on the unbaked crust and bake the pizza about 45 to 50 minutes.

Tip: Lining the Dutch oven with heavy-duty foil makes clean-up easy and also makes it a snap to lift the pizza out of the Dutch oven. If using foil, simply oil the foil as you would the Dutch oven.

ELEGANT DUTCH OVEN CHICKEN

Equipment:
10-inch Dutch oven
blender

Ingredients:
1/4 cup butter
1 teaspoon salt
1/2 teaspoon pepper
1 clove garlic, peeled and cut into pieces
3 large onions, sliced into rings
5 chicken breasts
paprika (for garnish)

Melt butter in the bottom of a 10-inch Dutch oven. Add salt, pepper, garlic and the onion rings. Place chicken pieces on top. Cover the Dutch oven and bake with medium to medium low heat for about 1 hour. Remove the chicken and puree the onion and butter mixture. Replace the chicken in the sauce and sprinkle with paprika. Serves 5.

CHICKEN FAJITAS

Ingredients:
2 pounds boneless, skinless chicken breasts
2 to 4 tablespoons dry fajita marinade mix
1/2 to 1 cup of water
1 onion, sliced
1 sweet red pepper, sliced in julienne strips
1 yellow pepper, sliced in julienne strips
1 medium-sized ripe tomato, chopped
8 (9-inch) flour tortillas
sour cream
guacamole (see recipe, page 88)

Cut the chicken into thin strips and place in a bowl or a large zip-top bag. Add marinade mix and enough water to dissolve the mix and coat the meat. Allow the chicken to marinate for 10 to 15 minutes before cooking. Heat a 12-inch Dutch oven over hot coals. Pour the meat and marinade into the hot Dutch oven and stir until marinade is mostly evaporated and meat is slightly browned. Add the vegetables to the Dutch oven. Stir them together with the meat, and allow to cook uncovered until the vegetables are cooked, but still firm. Meanwhile, place the lid of the Dutch oven upside-down over medium-heat coals. Place the tortillas on the lid to warm. (They may be placed on the lid in a stack and rotated so that all become warm, or placed on the lid 1 or 2 at a time as people are served.) Serve the fajitas by placing a small amount of the chicken and vegetables on the tortilla. Top with sour cream or guacamole as desired. Serve with Mexican Rice (see recipe, page 148). Serves 4 to 6.

ENCHILADA PIE

Ingredients:

2 pounds lean ground beef

1 medium onion, chopped

1 (10-3/4-ounce) can condensed tomato soup

2 (10-ounce) cans mild enchilada sauce

1 cup water

9 (8-inch) flour tortillas

1-1/2 to 2 cups (8 ounces) shredded Cheddar or
   Monterey Jack cheese

In 10- or 12-inch Dutch oven, brown the meat with the onion over hot coals. Drain off any grease or absorb it out with a paper towel. Add the soup, enchilada sauce and water. Simmer 5 minutes. Spoon 2/3 of the mixture into a medium bowl. Arrange 2 to 3 tortillas over the mixture remaining in the Dutch oven and sprinkle with cheese. Layer with half of the removed meat mixture, 2 or 3 more tortillas and cheese. Top with the remaining meat mixture and cheese. Bake for 10 to 15 minutes or until cheese melts and tortillas soften. Extra tortillas may be served with the enchilada pie as a side bread. Serves 6 to 8.

RED BEANS AND RICE

Ingredients:
1/2 cup converted rice, uncooked
1-1/2 cups water
1/2 teaspoon salt
1 onion, diced
1 (15-ounce) can red beans, drained
1 (15-ounce) can hot chili, no beans

Combine rice, water, salt and diced onion in a 10-inch Dutch oven. Simmer over medium heat for 15 to 20 minutes with lid on oven. Add beans and chili and stir. Cover the Dutch oven and bake with coals on top and bottom of oven for an additional 5 to 10 minutes. Serves 4.

BAKED BEANS

Ingredients:
1/2 pound center-cut bacon, cut into 1-inch pieces
1 onion, chopped
2 (30-ounce) cans pork and beans
1 green pepper, chopped
1 (14-ounce) bottle ketchup
1/4 cup brown sugar
1/4 cup dark molasses
2 tablespoons Worcestershire sauce

Brown the bacon in a 12-inch Dutch oven, then remove the bacon to a plate and drain off most of the grease. Brown the onion lightly in the remaining bacon grease, then add the cooked bacon and other ingredients. Spread out the coals under the Dutch oven and place coals on the lid. Cook at low heat for 15 to 20 minutes. Serves 12.

PULL-APART STICKY BUNS

Ingredients:
24 frozen dinner rolls
18-inch heavy-duty aluminum foil
2/3 cup brown sugar
2 teaspoons cinnamon
1/2 cup chopped pecans
1/2 cup butter, melted

Thaw the dinner rolls and snip each roll in half with a pair of scissors. Line a 12-inch Dutch oven with foil and lightly grease the foil. Mix the brown sugar, cinnamon and nuts in a bowl. Dip each roll in butter, then roll it in the cinnamon-sugar mixture and place in the Dutch oven. Sprinkle the remaining cinnamon-sugar mixture and butter over the rolls. Cover the Dutch oven and allow it to stand in a warm place until the rolls have risen to double in volume. Bake for 25 to 35 minutes. When rolls are done, invert the sticky buns onto a tray and peel back the foil. Serves 8 to 10.

CHERRY COBBLER

Ingredients:
18-inch heavy-duty aluminum foil
2 (20-ounce) cans cherry pie filling
1 yellow cake mix
1 (12-ounce) can lemon-lime soda pop

Line a 12-inch Dutch oven with foil. Pour in pie filling. Sprinkle cake mix evenly over filling. Pour pop over the cake mix. Stir gently to combine cake mix and pop only (not pie filling). Bake 35 minutes until top is golden brown. Serves 6 to 8.

PINEAPPLE UPSIDE-DOWN CAKE

Ingredients:

18-inch heavy-duty aluminum foil
1 (16-ounce) can pineapple slices
2 tablespoons butter or margarine
1 (8-ounce) jar maraschino cherries
1/2 cup packed brown sugar
1 (18-1/2-ounce) package yellow cake mix,
    prepared according to package directions

Line a 12-inch Dutch oven with foil. Drain pineapple, reserving juice. Place butter or margarine in the Dutch oven and place over low heat to melt. When butter is melted, arrange pineapple slices on top of foil and place a maraschino cherry in the center of each pineapple slice. Sprinkle brown sugar and 3 tablespoons of reserved juice over fruit. Pour prepared cake mix over the fruit. Put cover on Dutch oven. Bake with medium coals on top and bottom for 25 to 30 minutes or until a toothpick inserted in the center of the cake comes out clean. Cool 8 minutes in pan, away from heat, then invert the cake onto a platter. Carefully peel away the foil, and enjoy. Serves 6 to 8.

Stick and Spit Cooking

Stick and spit cooking conjure up visions of the Old West, but you don't have to saddle up to enjoy these delicious recipes. Just gather up your kinfolk and let everyone prepare their own meal just the way they like it. For more great ideas and tips on stick and spit cooking, please read chapter 8.

BARBECUE DRUMSTICKS

Ingredients:
1 pound ground beef
1 egg, beaten
1 small onion, chopped
1/4 cup barbecue sauce (recipe, page 82)
1 teaspoon salt
1/4 teaspoon pepper
bread crumbs
6 (3/4-inch) dowels
18-inch heavy-duty aluminum foil

Mix together the ground beef, egg, onion, barbecue sauce, salt and pepper. Divide into six equal portions. Form portions into 4-inch rectangular shapes around each dowel, then roll in bread crumbs. Place on a 12-by-18-inch piece of foil and wrap using the drugstore-wrap method (see pages 47 and 48), twisting the end of the foil around the dowel. Hold above coals or place on a wire grill 2 to 3 inches above the glowing coals. Cook for 15 to 20 minutes on each side. Serves 6.

APPLE ON A STICK

Ingredients:
2 cups sugar
2 tablespoons cinnamon
1 baking apple per person
3/4-inch dowel or roasting fork

Mix sugar and cinnamon together and place in a shallow bowl. Place apple on the end of a dowel or roasting fork and rotate over glowing coals until it becomes shiny and the skin begins to pop. Remove from fire, cool slightly and remove the skin from the apple. Roll in sugar and cinnamon, and place back over coals until the sugar begins to melt and drip off the apple. Remove apple from heat, cool slightly, slice and serve. (See photo, page 60.)

Variation: Apple Kabobs—Peel and core the apple and cut it into chunks. Place it on a skewer, brush with butter and roll in sugar and cinnamon. Toast over glowing coals.

KABOBS

Intriguing and taste-tempting kabobs can be served as a main dish, a side dish or even dessert. The nice thing about this method of cooking is that many different bite-sized foods can be arranged on serving plates and everyone can assemble his or her own favorite combinations. Some excellent kabob ingredients are listed below.

vegetables: peppers, zucchini, onions, summer squash, cherry tomatoes, black olives, green olives, small fresh mushrooms, marinated mushrooms, whole water chestnuts

vegetables requiring precooking: carrots, cauliflower, broccoli, fennel, potatoes

meats: marinated chunks or strips or beef, marinated chicken strips, marinated pork cubes, ham, sausage, meatballs, bacon

seafood: fish (monk fish, halibut, swordfish, tuna), oysters, shrimp, sea scallops

fruit and dessert items: apples, pineapple, peaches, bananas, maraschino cherries, orange quarters, doughnut holes, cut pieces of cake

A few tips for making and cooking kabobs:

Using skewers—If you are using bamboo skewers, soak them in water for at least an hour ahead of time. This will prevent them from scorching or catching fire. When using larger metal skewers, avoid using foods that may pop or split when placed on the skewer. To prevent foods from slipping off the skewer and becoming overcooked on one side, you can run two skewers parallel through all the foods. This makes the kabobs easier to turn and keeps odd-shaped or soft foods from slipping or falling off. Always use double skewers when cooking shrimp. Thread one skewer through the tail, and one through the head of each shrimp.

Selecting meats—Please see pages 60 and 61.

Choosing food combinations—Choose foods that require about the same cooking time. Combining foods that cook at different rates may result in part of the kabob burning and falling into the fire while the rest is still half-cooked. If you want to use foods that take little cooking, such as cherry tomatoes or bananas, with other longer-cooking foods, add the faster-cooking foods at the end of the cooking time, just a few minutes before you are ready to serve the kabobs. Alternatively, you might precook longer-cooking foods and just warm them up on the skewer.

Enhancing flavor and preventing scorching—Dry or nonoily foods may scorch on the edges while cooking. To prevent this, brush or spray the kabob with a lite cooking oil while it is cooking, or marinate the ingredients before placing them on the skewer. To enhance flavor, a simple flavored butter may be brushed on the kabobs just before serving. A simple flavored butter may be made by melting 1/4 cup butter or margarine and adding 3/4 teaspoon seasoned salt. Two more flavored butter recipes are given on the next page.

Knowing when foods are done—It is important to make sure that foods, especially meats, are properly cooked. Poultry and pork are done when they are no longer pink in the middle. Fish is done when it flakes easily with a fork. Sea scallops are done when they are white and no longer translucent. Shrimp is done when it is pink and firm.

LEMON BUTTER

Ingredients:
1/4 cup butter, melted
2 tablespoons lemon juice
2 teaspoons chopped fresh parsley

Add lemon juice and parsley to melted butter and brush over vegetable or seafood kabobs.

GINGER BUTTER

Ingredients:
1/4 cup butter
1 tablespoon sugar
1/4 teaspoon ginger

Melt all together and brush over fruits or dessert items.

LEMON ROSEMARY CHICKEN

Ingredients:
1 pound boneless, skinless chicken breasts
olive oil
zest of 1 lemon
1 teaspoon grated fresh ginger
1/2 teaspoon rosemary leaves
1/4 teaspoon onion powder
1/2 teaspoon salt
1/4 teaspoon pepper
skewers

Cut chicken breasts in half. Wash, pat dry and brush chicken with olive oil. Mix the lemon zest, ginger, rosemary, onion powder, salt and pepper, and coat each chicken piece with the seasoning rub. Place in the refrigerator for 20 minutes. Cut the chicken breasts into strips or chunks and thread on skewers. Cook over hot coals (about 4 inches from the coals) for 10 to 15 minutes, or until chicken is done. Serves 4.

SHRIMP AND BEEF KABOBS

Ingredients:
12 large fresh raw shrimp
1/4 cup soy sauce
1/2 pound sliced bacon, cut in half
1 pound tender beef, cut in cubes
2 oranges, divided into wedges

Peel and devein shrimp. Marinate shrimp in soy sauce for about 10 minutes, then wrap in halved bacon slices. Thread on double skewers, alternating with beef cubes and orange wedges. Cook over coals 15 to 20 minutes or until meat is cooked through. Serves 8 to 10.

PORK AND PINEAPPLE KABOBS

Ingredients:
1 pound pork tenderloin, cubed
15 to 20 chunks fresh or canned pineapple
2 apples, peeled and cut in bite-sized pieces
1 (5-ounce) bottle tiny cocktail onions
1/4 cup melted butter

Thread meat, fruits, and onions in desired order on skewer. Brush with butter. Cook over hot coals 20 to 25 minutes, until pork is cooked through. Makes 8 to 10 kabobs.

STUFFED MUSHROOM KABOBS

Ingredients:
18 to 20 medium-sized button mushrooms
1 (2-1/2-ounce) can deviled ham
20 pearl onions
9 to 10 cherry tomatoes
cooking oil
melted or seasoned butter (optional)

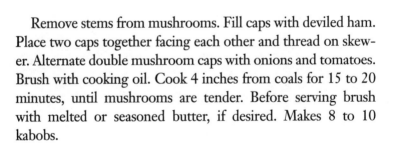

Remove stems from mushrooms. Fill caps with deviled ham. Place two caps together facing each other and thread on skewer. Alternate double mushroom caps with onions and tomatoes. Brush with cooking oil. Cook 4 inches from coals for 15 to 20 minutes, until mushrooms are tender. Before serving brush with melted or seasoned butter, if desired. Makes 8 to 10 kabobs.

HAWAIIAN HAM AND CHEESE KABOBS

Ingredients:
8 to 10 thin slices of ham, cut in 1-inch strips
1/4 pound Swiss cheese, cut in cubes
15 to 20 chunks fresh or canned pineapple
green olives (optional)

Wrap ham strips around cubes of cheese and thread onto a skewer, alternating with pineapple chunks. Add green olives, if desired. Cook 3 to 4 inches above hot coals for approximately 5 minutes. When cheese is melted and starts dripping, kabob is done. Makes about 6 kabobs.

ITALIAN PORK KABOBS

Ingredients:
1-1/2 pounds pork, cut in 1-inch cubes
1 (8-ounce) bottle Italian dressing or 1 cup vinaigrette
  dressing (recipe, page 83)
12 fresh button mushrooms
6 Roma or plum tomatoes, cut in wedges
1 medium zucchini, cut in 1-inch pieces

Marinate pork in the Italian or vinaigrette dressing at least 2 hours in the refrigerator. Thread on skewer, alternating with vegetables. Cook 4 inches from heat for 20 to 25 minutes, until pork is cooked through. Makes about 6 kabobs.

SWORDFISH OR TUNA KABOBS

Ingredients:
1-1/2 pounds swordfish or fresh tuna, cubed
1 cup vinaigrette dressing (recipe, page 83)
1 green pepper
1 red pepper
1 yellow pepper

1 red onion, cut in chunks
1 Roma or plum tomato, cut in quarters

Marinate the fish cubes in vinaigrette dressing. Wash and seed the peppers and cut in squares. Prepare the other vegetables. Thread the fish on skewers, alternating with the vegetables. Grill 4 inches from the heat for 15 to 20 minutes, or until fish is the desired doneness. Makes 6 to 8 kabobs.

OYSTER ROLL-UP KABOBS

Ingredients:
20 smoked oysters
1/2 pound lean center-cut bacon slices, cut in half
3 ounces ripe olives

Wrap oysters in half-slices of bacon and skewer alternately with olives. Cook over hot coals until bacon is done. Makes 8 to 10 kabobs.

CHERRY-COCONUT CAKE KABOBS

Ingredients:
1 small pound cake, cut in cubes
1 (8-ounce) jar apricot, strawberry or cherry jam or preserves
1 cup shredded coconut
1 (8-ounce) jar maraschino cherries

Spread jam on all sides of cubes of pound cake. Roll in coconut. Thread cake cubes on skewer alternating with maraschino cherries. Roast over coals until coconut is browned. Makes 6 to 8 kabobs.

CHERRY-PEACH KABOBS

Ingredients:
6 to 8 peach halves (canned or fresh, peeled)
maraschino cherries
7 to 10 pineapple chunks (canned or fresh)
melted butter or ginger butter (recipe, page 129)

Quarter peach halves. Thread fruit onto double skewers, beginning and ending skewer with pineapple chunks. Cook over coals until warmed through, brushing often with butter. Makes 4 to 6 kabobs.

BANANA-NUT KABOBS

Ingredients:
4 bananas, peeled and cut in quarters
1/4 cup melted butter
4 to 8 maraschino cherries (optional)
1/2 cup mixed chopped nuts (peanuts, walnuts and pecans)

Dip bananas in melted butter and thread on skewers. Add cherries, if desired. Roast over coals until warmed through, then roll in chopped nuts and serve. Makes 4 kabobs.

Breads

Baking bread outdoors? That's right—you don't need a conventional oven to "rise" to the occasion of bread baking. Give these recipes a try and you'll really be on a "roll."

ROASTED GARLIC ON FRENCH

Ingredients:
1 garlic head
olive oil
salt
ground black pepper
1 loaf French bread, sliced

Slice off the top of the head of garlic, making sure that part of each clove is exposed. Brush the tops of the cloves with olive oil and sprinkle with salt and pepper. Place in a ceramic garlic baker or wrap in foil. Bake in a 275°F oven for 1 hour. Remove the garlic, brush the top again with oil and bake for 1/2 to 1 hour more. Garlic cloves should be soft, but still pop out of the skin when squeezed. Place cloves on slices of bread and spread the soft garlic. Sprinkle with salt and pepper, as desired.

Variation: Garlic can also be roasted in a microwave oven. Prepare the garlic head as above and place it in a ceramic garlic baker. Cook on high for 2 to 3 minutes.

Tip: Heat French bread before or after spreading with garlic by wrapping the loaf in foil and placing it on a rack above coals or in a closed, heated grill for 20 to 30 minutes.

BREAD ON A STICK

Ingredients:

1 (1-pound) loaf frozen bread dough, thawed, or
   1 (1-pound) loaf bread dough
1/4 cup flour
1/4 cup melted butter or margarine
4 tablespoons Parmesan cheese
1 teaspoon seasoned salt
4 (1-inch) dowels
1 tablespoon vegetable oil

Using a sharp knife, cut the dough into six pieces. Roll each piece in flour and then form them into long, thin pieces. Dip each piece of dough in melted butter, then roll it in Parmesan cheese. Sprinkle with seasoned salt. Wash the ends of the dowels and oil each one about 6 inches at one end. Starting at that end, twist the bread around the dowel, making sure that the end is covered and that the twists meet so that the dowel is covered. Bake the bread by rotating it over hot coals for 10 to 20 minutes. Slide the bread off the end of the stick and fill the hollow inside with cheese, spaghetti sauce, butter or salsa. Makes 6 large rolls. (See photo, page 60.)

Variation: Roll the uncooked dough in butter, then in cinnamon sugar. Fill the inside of the cooked bread with applesauce, jam or pudding.

BRICK BISCUITS

Equipment:
4 to 6 bricks
wheelbarrow grill
briquets
hand broom

When you use your wheelbarrow as a grill, fill it first with dirt, then cover the dirt with bricks. Cook with hot charcoal on top of the bricks. When you are finished cooking your main dishes, move the coals to one side, dust the ashes off the bricks and use the hot bricks to cook these biscuits! See photos, page 5.

Ingredients:

2 cups biscuit mix
1/2 cup water
nonstick cooking spray

Mix biscuit mix and water to form a soft dough. Pinch off a small portion of dough and pat or roll it into a flat, round, pancake-like shape. The thinner the biscuit, the faster it will cook. Lightly spray the bricks with nonstick cooking spray. Lay the biscuits on the hot bricks and cook until done, turning once. Serve plain or with butter and jam or jelly. Makes 10 to 12 medium-sized biscuits.

Salads

You'll never look at salads the same way again after tossing together these recipes. From the simple to the exquisite—they're all easy to make and even easier to eat.

PINEAPPLE BOATS

Ingredients:
1 fresh pineapple
1 (4-ounce) bottle maraschino cherries

Cut fresh pineapple in quarters lengthwise without removing crown. Using a crescent-shaped grapefruit knife, cut between fruit and rind of one quarter, starting at the stem end. Then slice between the fruit and the core, also starting at the stem end. This will detach the quarter of fruit but leave the core, rind and crown intact. Slide the fruit out of the rind and cut it into 4 to 6 slices. Slide the slices back into the core. Slightly push each slice in alternating directions in the pineapple core. Skewer each slice with a toothpick and maraschino cherry for easy eating. Repeat this process with the other 3 quarters of the pineapple. Serves 6 to 8. May be used as an appetizer.

PICNIC PUDDING SALAD

Ingredients:
1 (20-ounce) can pineapple chunks with juice
2 bananas, sliced
1 cup shredded coconut
1 (11-ounce) can mandarin oranges, drained
1 (16-ounce) can fruit cocktail with juice
1 (3-3/4-ounce) package instant lemon pudding mix

Chill the canned fruits. In medium bowl, combine pineapple chunks and juice with bananas, coconut, oranges, and fruit cocktail with juice. Stirring slowly, sprinkle pudding mix into fruit mixture. Let stand 5 minutes. Pudding will set in fruit juice. Makes 6-1/2 cups.

WATERMELON BASKET FRESH
FRUIT SALAD

Ingredients:
1/2 ripe honeydew melon
juice of 2 limes
2 pears, cut in small chunks
1/2 ripe cantaloupe
1 large watermelon
1 bunch red table grapes, washed and removed from stems
1 basket strawberries, washed and halved or quartered
juice of 3 oranges
1 lemon or lime for garnish (optional)
extra grapes for garnish (optional)

Make melon balls from the honeydew half using a melon-baller or very small ice cream scoop. Toss in a bowl with the lime juice and pear chunks. Melon-ball the cantaloupe. Cut the watermelon into a basket shape (see instructions below), and cut the removed watermelon into chunks, removing the seeds. Toss the watermelon, cantaloupe, grapes, strawberries, and orange juice together with the honeydew and pears. Return fruit to the watermelon basket to serve. Garnish the basket with citrus slices or extra bunches of grapes. (See photos, page 25.) Serves 8 to 10.

Variation: You can make this same salad and serve it in a glass bowl. If you are doing this, you can use the following method to remove the seeds from the watermelon.

Cut both ends off the watermelon and set it on its end inside a large dish to catch the juice. Place the point of a paring knife just into the seeds and cut the watermelon from top to bottom, about 3 inches deep. Repeat all the way around the watermelon, creating wedges about 3 to 4 inches apart. With the palm of your hand, hit the melon up and down along each wedge until the wedges are loose. The seed base is the weakest point of the watermelon, and with a little encouragement, the outside layer will naturally separate from the heart of the melon at the seed layer. Remove the wedges and scrape out the watermelon seeds.

Instructions for Watermelon Basket: (For pictures showing the completed watermelon, please see page 25.) Set the watermelon on a table or a counter to determine what side should be the bottom. Place it so that it sits firmly on its base. Place a strip of 1-inch masking tape around the watermelon, going around the long way at the center. Place two strips of tape over the top of the watermelon, starting at the center of the tape you just put on. This tape marks where the handle will be, so it should be perpendicular to the base. Begin cutting the watermelon with a sharp paring knife, cutting above the tape going around the long way. Begin at the point where the handle marking tape makes a corner with the tape going around the watermelon. When you reach this same corner on the other side, stop, and cut outside the tape marking the handle. About 1/4 of the watermelon has just been cut free and you should be able to remove that section by inserting a knife in the crack and using it to pry out the piece. You may cut the watermelon in a straight line as described above, or make a zigzag edge by inserting the paring knife at alternating angles as you cut. Repeat the above process for the other side of the watermelon basket. When you have removed the rind to create the basket shape, use a large spoon to scoop the melon out and hollow out the handle. Hollow out the base of the "basket" about 1/3 of the way down.

MARINATED CARROT SALAD

Ingredients:
5 cups (2 pounds) fresh carrots, cut in thick round slices
1 large onion, sliced in thin rounds
1 large green pepper, chopped
1 (10-3/4-ounce) can tomato soup
1/3 cup salad oil
1/2 cup sugar
3/4 cup vinegar
1 tablespoon prepared mustard
2 tablespoons Worcestershire sauce
1 teaspoon garlic powder
1 teaspoon salt

Cook carrots in boiling water until they are cooked, but still crunchy. Drain and cool. Mix with all other ingredients. Refrigerate 12 hours. Serves 10.

WARM GOAT CHEESE SALAD

Ingredients:
3 ripe tomatoes
6 to 8 ounces goat cheese
1 tablespoon olive oil
2 tablespoons fresh basil, chopped
ground black pepper
1 small head lettuce or 3 cups salad greens (any kind)

Slice the tomatoes in 1/4-inch slices and spread out on a baking sheet. Mix the goat cheese, oil and chopped fresh basil to form a paste. Place 2 tablespoons of the goat cheese mixture on each slice of tomato and pepper lightly. Place under broiler just long enough for the cheese to melt. Serve 2 slices of tomato per person on top of salad greens. Serves 6.

TOMATO MOZZARELLA PLATE

Ingredients:
1 small head lettuce or 4 cups salad greens (any kind)
4 tomatoes (16 tomato slices)
1/2 pound fresh mozzarella, cut in 1/4-inch slices
vinaigrette dressing (recipe, page 83)
2 to 3 tablespoons chopped basil

Wash the lettuce or greens and arrange the leaves on a medium-sized plate or tray. Lay the tomato and mozzarella slices alternating across the plate in a line or in a circle. Drizzle vinaigrette dressing over the whole and sprinkle with basil. Serves 6 to 8.

Note: Fresh mozzarella is softer than packaged mozzarella. It usually comes packed in liquid and can be obtained in the deli section of your grocery store.

RICE VEGETABLE SALAD

Ingredients:
2 cups uncooked rice
1 cup black beans (canned or precooked and drained)
1/2 red pepper, chopped
1/2 green pepper, chopped
1/2 cup chopped parsley
1/2 cup chopped cilantro
1 tablespoon chopped fresh tarragon
1/2 cup lemon juice
1/3 cup olive oil
1/3 cup dried cranberries (optional)

Cook the rice according to package directions. Combine rice and beans with all other ingredients. Stir and chill. Best if made the night before. Serves 6.

GERMAN POTATO SALAD

Ingredients:

4 new red potatoes (small)
4 new white potatoes (small)
1 clove garlic
2 teaspoons salt
1/2 teaspoon pepper
10 slices bacon
1 onion, diced
2 tablespoons flour
1 (14-1/2-ounce) can chicken broth
1/4 cup red wine vinegar
3 green onions, chopped
4 tablespoons chopped parsley
1/2 teaspoon salt
dash of pepper

Cut potatoes into quarters and place in pan. Peel garlic and cut the clove into quarters. Place in pan with potatoes along with salt and 1/2 teaspoon pepper. Cover potatoes with water and boil 20 to 25 minutes until they are tender. Drain and set aside to cool. Cut bacon into pieces and fry until crispy. Drain on a paper towel, saving 2 teaspoons of bacon grease. In the same frying pan place diced onion. Cook in bacon grease until browned. Sprinkle flour over the onions and stir well. Slowly add in the chicken broth. Add green onions, parsley, vinegar, salt and pepper. Simmer 10 to 20 minutes. Cut potatoes into bite-sized pieces. Stir sauce into the potatoes and serve warm. Serves 6 to 8.

Note: This recipe also works well and is delicious prepared in a Dutch oven.

TRADITIONAL POTATO SALAD

Ingredients:

3 to 4 pounds potatoes
2 cloves garlic, peeled and cut in half
2 teaspoons salt
1/4 cup pickle juice
4 hard boiled eggs
1 cup diced dill pickles
1 cup diced celery
1/4 cup chopped green onion
1/2 teaspoon salt
1/4 teaspoon pepper
1/2 teaspoon onion powder (optional)
1 to 1-1/2 cups low-fat or regular mayonnaise
extra salt and pepper, as desired
dash of paprika

Cut potatoes in quarters and place in a cooking pot with 2 cloves garlic and 2 teaspoons salt. Cover with water and bring to a boil, then lower heat and simmer until potatoes are done. (Potatoes should be soft, but still firm.) Drain the potatoes and refrigerate to cool. When potatoes are cool, remove peels then cut potatoes into bite-sized chunks. Place in a bowl and pour the pickle juice over the potatoes. Chop 3 of the 4 hard boiled eggs and add to the potatoes, along with the chopped vegetables, salt, pepper, onion powder (if desired) and mayonnaise. Toss salad together and refrigerate for several hours or overnight. Add extra salt and pepper, as desired. Garnish the top of the salad with remaining slices of hard-boiled egg and a dash of paprika. Serves 8 to 10.

ITALIAN PASTA SALAD

Ingredients:

1 large red onion
1 red pepper, cut in quarters
1 yellow pepper, cut in quarters
1 zucchini
3 cups cooked pasta (rainbow rotini or fuselli)
1 cup vinaigrette dressing (recipe, page 83)
2 tablespoons fresh basil, chopped
2 cups broccoli and cauliflower florets, cooked, but still firm
1 (6-ounce) jar marinated artichoke hearts, drained
1/2 cup grated Parmesan or Romano cheese

Grill the onion, peppers and zucchini according to instructions for grilled vegetables (see page 104). After vegetables are grilled, cut them into bite-sized pieces. Toss grilled vegetables and all other ingredients together. Best if made several hours ahead and refrigerated so flavors have time to blend. Serves 8 to 10.

GOURMET GREEN SALAD

Ingredients:
1 small head lettuce
1 cup celery, diced
1/2 cup diced green onion
1 (10-ounce) package frozen peas, thawed
1 (6-ounce) can sliced water chestnuts, drained
1/2 cup lite mayonnaise
1-1/2 cups lite dairy sour cream
1/2 cup grated Parmesan cheese
1/4 cup crumbled, cooked bacon

Break lettuce into pieces and place in bottom of a round serving dish. Layer celery, green onions, peas and water chestnuts. In a small bowl, mix mayonnaise and sour cream. Spread over vegetables. Sprinkle Parmesan cheese and bacon on top. Cover with plastic and refrigerate overnight. Toss before serving. Serves 6 to 8.

BABY GREENS SALAD

Ingredients:
1 pound baby salad greens
1/2 cup vinaigrette dressing (recipe, page 83)
feta or Parmesan cheese
grated mixed nuts (optional)

Place greens on individual salad plates and drizzle with vinaigrette dressing, or toss greens with vinaigrette dressing in a serving bowl immediately before serving. Sprinkle greens with grated Parmesan cheese or crumbled feta cheese and with grated nuts as desired. Serves 6 to 8.

Veggies and Side Dishes

No one will have to remind your guests to eat their vegetables when you serve these on the side. These dishes will complement your meal, and some can even stand on their own!

OVEN-ROASTED POTATOES

Ingredients:
10 new potatoes, quartered
2 red onions, cut in 1/2-inch slices
vinaigrette dressing (recipe, page 83)
casserole dish or baking pan

Preheat oven to 400 or 425°F. Coat the potatoes and onions with the vinaigrette dressing and spread out in the casserole dish. Bake for 35 to 45 minutes or until potatoes are toasted and cooked through. Serves 5 to 6.

LOW-FAT, HIGH-TASTE FRENCH FRIES

Ingredients:
5 potatoes
3 egg whites
1 to 2 tablespoons salad blend seasoning

Peel potatoes and cut into french fries. Whisk egg whites until frothy. Toss potatoes in egg whites and place on a lightly oiled pan. Sprinkle seasoning over the fries and bake at 375°F for 40 minutes. Serves 4 to 6.

SAFFRON RICE

Ingredients:
1/2 onion, diced
2 tablespoons butter or margarine
2 chicken bouillon cubes
3 cups rice
5 cups water
pinch of saffron

Preheat oven to 375°F. Brown the onion in the butter or margarine in a casserole dish with a lid or Dutch oven. Add chicken bouillon cubes and rice and stir together. Add water and saffron and stir. Cover and bake for 20 minutes. Remove from oven and stir. Replace the lid and bake for 10 more minutes. Serves 8 to 10.

MEXICAN RICE

Ingredients:
1 small onion, chopped
2 tablespoons vegetable oil
1 cup long-grain rice
2 cups canned tomatoes, diced
water to make 2 cups
2 tablespoons chopped fresh parsley or cilantro
1 tablespoon taco seasoning
salt and pepper, as desired

Brown onion in the oil over hot coals in a 10-inch Dutch oven. Add rice and brown it while stirring. Drain juice from tomatoes into a measuring container and add water to make 2 cups liquid total. Add liquid, tomatoes and seasonings to the rice and onion. Place lid on Dutch oven and cook with medium heat for about 20 to 25 minutes. Serves 6 to 8.

BAKED YAMS

Ingredients:
2 large yams
cinnamon
butter or margarine, as desired
salt and pepper, as desired

Cut yams in half crosswise and bake for 40 to 60 minutes in a 425°F oven, or for 60 to 90 minutes outdoors in a Dutch oven. They may also be baked over coals wrapped in foil. When yams are soft in the middle, cut them in half again down their length and score the flesh of each piece with a fork. Sprinkle each piece with cinnamon and serve with butter or margarine, salt and pepper. Serves 6 to 8. These are especially good served with barbecued ribs or pork chops.

BAKED POTATO BAR

Ingredients:
large baking potatoes
potato toppings (see suggestions below)

Wash the potatoes and bake them at 375°F for 45 to 60 minutes, or until done. (Potatoes are done when a fork slides into the potato easily.) Slit each potato lengthwise and serve buffet style, allowing guests to add their own toppings. Depending on the toppings, this can serve as a side dish or a one-dish meal.

Suggested toppings:

- butter or margarine
- salt and pepper
- onion salt
- sliced green onions
- Italian-style dressing
- Parmesan cheese
- chili con carne
- mushroom sauce
- steamed broccoli florets
- bacon bits

- whipped butter
- salad blend seasoning
- snipped chives
- ranch-style dressing
- grated Cheddar cheese
- sour cream
- spaghetti sauce
- cream of mushroom soup
- cheese sauce
- chopped black olives

GARLIC-BROILED CROOKNECK SQUASH

Ingredients:
2 yellow crookneck squash
garlic salt
1/4 cup fresh grated Parmesan cheese
2 tablespoons butter

Slice the squash in 1/4- to 1/2-inch slices lengthwise, or diagonally crosswise. Lay the slices on a lightly greased cookie sheet. Sprinkle each slice with garlic salt and Parmesan cheese. Place a small piece of butter on each slice. Bake at 400°F for 8 to 10 minutes on the top oven rack. Serve immediately. Serves 4.

Variation: Squash may be cooked similarly in a frying pan or on a grill.

SUMMER SQUASH CASSEROLE

Ingredients:
6 to 7 medium yellow squash, sliced (6 cups)
1 large onion, chopped
1 can cream of chicken soup
1 cup dairy sour cream
1 cup grated raw carrot
1 (8-ounce) package seasoned stuffing mix
1/2 cup melted butter or margarine

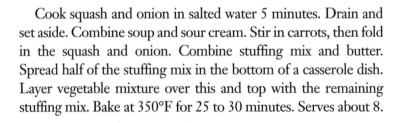

Cook squash and onion in salted water 5 minutes. Drain and set aside. Combine soup and sour cream. Stir in carrots, then fold in the squash and onion. Combine stuffing mix and butter. Spread half of the stuffing mix in the bottom of a casserole dish. Layer vegetable mixture over this and top with the remaining stuffing mix. Bake at 350°F for 25 to 30 minutes. Serves about 8.

Tip: For a lower-fat recipe, make as above, but leave out the butter or margarine. Use low-fat sour cream and soup.

Desserts

When it comes time to satisfy that sweet tooth, do it with flair! These tasty treats are almost as much fun to make as they are to eat.

SPONGE CAKE WITH FRUIT

Ingredients:

2 oranges
1 angel food cake
3 bananas, sliced
1 (20-ounce) can of chunk pineapple, with juice
1 (7-ounce) package shredded coconut
1 cup heavy cream
2 tablespoons sugar

Using a sharp serrated knife, cut the rind off the oranges. Cut the oranges into 1/2-inch slices, cutting across the sections, and then separate the segments to make small orange pieces. Cut the angel food cake into slices. Mix the fruits together. Put pieces of cake on dessert plates and place a large spoonful of the fruit mixture on each slice. Begin whipping the cream and then add the sugar to the cream. Add a dollop of whipped cream on top of each piece of cake. Serves about 12.

MACAROON COOKIES

Ingredients:

3 eggs
1 (14-ounce) package finely shredded coconut
1 cup sugar
2 tablespoons butter or margarine, softened

Beat eggs well, then add other ingredients and mix well. Scoop dough with a 1/4-cup measure and roll into balls. Place onto a greased cookie sheet, leaving a little space between each cookie. Bake at 350°F for 10 to 15 minutes or until golden brown.

Variation: For a snack-sized macaroon, scoop the dough with a 1/8-cup measure. Bake as above.

VOLCANO CAKE

Ingredients:
1 chocolate or other flavor bundt cake, baked
1 (29-ounce) can cherry pie filling
1/4 to 1/2 pound dry ice
3 Solo Ultra Clear™ (9-ounce) plastic cups

Spoon the cherry pie filling on top of the bundt cake. Place several small chips of dry ice in two of the plastic cups. Leave the third plastic cup empty and place it in the hollow center of the cake. Just before serving, pour very hot water over the dry ice in one cup. Place this cup inside the empty cup in the center of the cake. This will make the volcano "steam!" If the steam slows down, replace the first cup of dry ice with the other cup and add hot water. (The empty cup in the hollow of the cake makes for easy switching of the cups containing dry ice.) Serves 10 to 12.

Tips on using dry ice: You can break a block of dry ice into small chips by hitting the block with a hammer. Remember to **ALWAYS** use gloves when handling dry ice! Never touch dry ice with bare skin. Placing the dry ice in water will make it steam; the hotter the water, the more steam the dry ice will produce.

Variation: Place small flags and lighted tapered candles in the cake for a festive Independence Day celebration cake. (See picture, page 69.)

PUDDING CONES

Ingredients:
1 (3-ounce) package instant pudding mix—any flavor
milk or water
1 cup whipped topping or whipped cream
4 to 6 flat-bottomed ice cream cones

Make pudding according to package directions, using 1/4 cup less milk or water than the package calls for. Blend in 1 cup whipped topping or whipped cream. Serve the pudding in the cones. Serves 4 to 6.

Tip: For away-from-home Pudding Cones, mix the pudding in a zip-top bag by sealing and then shaking or squeezing the bag. Cut off a corner to dispense the pudding into the cones.

DIRT DESSERT

Ingredients:
1 large (5-1/2-ounce) package instant chocolate pudding mix
3 cups cold milk
1 (8-ounce) container frozen whipped topping, thawed
1 (6-ounce) package miniature chocolate chips
1 large package chocolate sandwich cookies
1 toy wheelbarrow, cleaned and lined with foil
Gummi worms, for garnish

Mix the pudding mix and milk according to the package directions and allow to set for a few minutes. Fold in the whipped topping and chocolate chips. Crush the sandwich cookies to crumb consistency. Put half the pudding mixture in the wheelbarrow. Top with half of the cookie crumbs. Layer with the rest of the pudding and top with cookie crumbs. Chill the dessert. Before serving, add the gummi worms on top of the wheelbarrow dessert. (See picture, page 70.) Serves 6 to 8.

Variation: Make the dessert as above, except layer the dessert in 6 (8-ounce) plastic cups. Top each cup with crumbs as described above and place a silk or paper flower in each "flowerpot." Serves 6.

SAND BUCKET DESSERT

Ingredients:
1 large (5-1/2-ounce) package instant vanilla pudding mix
3 cups cold milk
1 (8-ounce) container frozen whipped topping, thawed
1 large package vanilla sandwich cookies or vanilla wafers
1 clean toy sand bucket with shovel
3 gumdrops for each "ant"
1 toothpick for each "ant"
2 (1/2-inch) pieces thin black rope licorice for each "ant"

Mix the pudding mix and milk according to package directions and allow to set for a few minutes. Fold in the whipped topping. Crush the cookies to crumb consistency. Put half the pudding mixture in the sand bucket and top with half of the cookie crumbs. Layer with the rest of the pudding and top with cookie crumbs. Chill the dessert. Make sand ants out of gumdrops and toothpicks by pushing 3 gumdrops onto a toothpick. Break the toothpick to match the length of the gumdrops. Add 2 small pieces of rope licorice to make antennae. Place the ants on top of the dessert and serve with a clean sand shovel. Serves 6 to 8.

Variation: Make the dessert as above, except layer the dessert in 6 (8-ounce) plastic cups. Top each cup with crumbs as described above and a sand ant. Make each cup into an individual "sand bucket" by adding a "handle" made from a pipe cleaner or a 1/2-inch strip of fun foam. Add a plastic spoon for a "shovel." Yields 6 individual servings.

HOMEMADE FROZEN YOGURT DELIGHT

Ingredients:
8 cups lemon or vanilla yogurt
1/2 cup frozen juice concentrate (orange or lemon)

Mix well, then freeze in ice-cream freezer. Makes about 2 quarts frozen yogurt.

DELICIOUS ICE CREAM

Ingredients:
2 oranges, peeled
2 lemons, peeled
2 cups sugar
2 cups milk
2 cups heavy cream

Place peeled fruits in blender and whip until relatively smooth. Add sugar and blend. Stir in the milk and cream and place in ice cream freezer. Freeze according to ice cream freezer instructions. Makes about 1-1/2 quarts ice cream.

TIN-CAN ICE CREAM

Equipment:
1 (1 pound) coffee can with lid, well-cleaned
1 (#10 can) with lid
1 (8-pound) bag of ice, crushed or in cubes
3/4 cup rock salt
table knife

Ingredients:
3/4 cup milk
1 cup whipping cream
1/3 cup sugar
1/2 teaspoon vanilla extract

Put all ingredients in the 1-pound coffee can with a tight-fitting plastic lid. Place lid on can. Place can with ingredients inside a #10 can with a tight-fitting plastic lid. Pack larger can with crushed ice around smaller can. Pour at least 1/2 cup of rock salt evenly over ice. Place lid on #10 can. Roll back and forth on cement slab or other flat surface for 10 minutes. Open outer can. Remove inner can with ingredients and open. Use a table knife to stir up mixture and scrape sides of can. If ice cream is not frozen hard enough, replace the lid. Drain ice water from larger can. Insert smaller can; pack with more ice and rest of salt. Roll back and forth for 5 more minutes. Makes about 3 cups ice cream.

BALL-TOSS ICE CREAM

Equipment:
2 (1-quart) zip-top bags
2 (1-gallon) zip-top bags
1 (8-pound) bag of ice, crushed or in cubes
1/2 cup rock salt
newspaper
heavy-duty strapping or packaging tape

Ingredients:
3/4 cup whole milk or flavored milk
1 cup whipping cream
1/3 cup sugar
1/2 teaspoon vanilla extract

Place all ingredients in a 1-quart bag. Squeeze out all the air and seal the bag. Place this bag inside the other quart bag and seal. Place the double-bagged ice cream mix inside a gallon zip-top bag. Fill the gallon-size bag with ice, sprinkle the ice with the rock salt and seal the bag. Place this bag inside the other gallon bag and seal. Wrap the filled bags in several layers of newspaper. Secure the newspaper by wrapping it with heavy-duty tape. Tape the "ball" on all sides so that it will hold its shape. Now, toss the "ice cream ball" back and forth for 15 to 20 minutes. Unwrap the ball, remove the ice and enjoy the ice cream! Makes about 3 cups.

Appendix

PRODUCE	DAIRY	MEAT
FROZEN	CANNED	BAKERY
DRY GOODS	HOUSEHOLD SUPPLIES	MISC.

Low-Calorie Substitutions

When you want delicious meals that are nutritious and low in calories, try substituting one food for another.

INSTEAD OF	TRY
Spaghetti	Bean sprouts French-cut green beans Spaghetti squash (a tasty low-calorie food)
Mayonnaise	Yogurt (especially good in salad dressings)
Sour cream	Low-calorie imitation sour cream; plain, low-fat yogurt; low-fat cottage cheese, blended smooth
Whipped cream	Non-dairy topping; chilled evaporated milk (whipped)
Whole milk	Skim, 2%, or 1% butterfat milk, or nonfat dry milk (reconstituted)

Emergency Substitutions

There's nothing worse than running out of a crucial ingredient in the middle of a recipe. If it happens to you, try one of these suggestions:

1 cup cake flour =
2 tablespoons cornstarch, then fill with all-purpose flour to one cup

1 teaspoon dry mustard =
1 tablespoon prepared mustard

1 cup butter or margarine =
1 cup shortening and 1/2 teaspoon salt

1 cup corn syrup =
1 cup sugar and 1/4 cup water

1 cup buttermilk =
1 cup milk and 1 tablespoon white vinegar

1 cup nuts =
1 cup Grapenuts cereal and 1/4 teaspoon almond flavoring

1 cup light cream =
1 cup undiluted evaporated milk

1 (15-ounce) can tomato sauce =
1 (6-ounce) can tomato paste and 3/4 cup water

1 tablespoon cornstarch (for thickening) =
2 tablespoons all-purpose flour

1 teaspoon baking powder =
1/2 teaspoon cream of tartar and 1/4 teaspoon baking soda

1 ounce unsweetened chocolate =
3 tablespoons cocoa powder and 1 tablespoon
butter or margarine

1 cup molasses =
1 cup honey (taste is milder)

1 cup honey =
1-1/2 cups sugar and 1/4 cup water

1 cup sour cream (for baking) =
7/8 cup buttermilk and 3 tablespoons butter

1 cup heavy cream (for baking) =
1/3 cup melted butter or margarine and
3/4 cup milk

1 cup ketchup or chili sauce =
1 cup tomato sauce, 1/4 cup sugar and
2 tablespoons vinegar

1 cup tomato paste =
1 cup tomato sauce plus 2 tablespoons
all-purpose flour

How Much Is Enough?

When the recipe calls for a cup of sliced apples or a cup of bread crumbs or cracker crumbs, how do you know whether you have enough? Here's a handy chart to help you.

1 cup fine cracker crumbs =
> 28 soda crackers

1/3 cup dry bread crumbs =
> 1 slice toast

2/3 cup soft bread crumbs =
> 1 slice fresh bread

4 cups all-purpose flour =
> 1 pound

6-3/4 cups cooked rice =
> 1 pound uncooked rice

4 cups cooked spaghetti =
> 8 ounces uncooked spaghetti

3 cups cooked noodles =
> 4 ounces uncooked noodles

8 cups cooked macaroni =
> 1 pound

2-1/2 cups + 2 tablespoons shortening =
> 1 pound

1 cup egg whites =
> 8 large egg whites

1 cup grated Parmesan cheese =
> 3 ounces grated cheese

2-1/4 cups cottage cheese =
1 pound

4 cups shredded Cheddar cheese =
1 pound

2 cups cocoa =
8 ounces

2-1/4 cups granulated sugar =
1 pound

2-1/4 cups firmly packed brown sugar =
1 pound

2-1/2 cups chopped walnuts =
1 pound of shelled walnuts

1/2 cup chopped onion =
1 medium onion, chopped

1-1/4 cups ketchup =
14 ounces

1 cup chopped apple =
1 large apple, chopped

8 cups pared sliced apples (or 5 to 6 cups applesauce) =
3 pounds of apples

1 pound apples =
3 medium apples

1-1/4 cups chopped dates =
8 ounces pitted dates

1/4 to 1/3 cup orange juice =
juice of 1 large orange

2 to 3 tablespoons lemon =
   juice of one lemon

1-1/2 cups mashed bananas =
   2 large bananas (1 pound)

2-2/3 cups cut-up dried figs =
   1 pound dried figs

TIDBITS FOR CREATIVE COOKS

1. If celery or carrots go limp before you use them, soak in cold water one hour. Add lemon juice or vinegar. Drain vegetables. Place in plastic bag and put in refrigerator until crisp.

2. For quick croutons, butter bread and sprinkle with spices such as sage, thyme, garlic salt or oregano. Cut into cubes and toast under broiler, stirring occasionally for even browning. Use in salads, soups or vegetables. Or use in dressings with meat.

3. To soften dried pastry, place in airtight container for 24 hours with slice of fresh bread.

4. Place hard brown sugar in airtight container for 24 hours for sugar to soften

5. Cookies too soft? Heat them in a 300°F oven for five minutes. Too hard? Place in an air-tight container overnight with slice of fresh bread or apple slices.

6. Broil stale potato chips for a few minutes to restore freshness. Do not brown.

7. Place soggy crackers or cereal on baking sheet and heat a few minutes in the oven.

8. Grate hardened cheese for casseroles and pizza.

9. Before thawing old frozen vegetables, run boiling water over them. Drain all liquid and cook in fresh water. Add to soups or stews, or cook in broth.

10. If turkey tastes dry, sprinkle with water, cover with foil and heat. Serve with gravy over it.

11. For cream that will not whip, add an egg white and chill. Try again.

12. To remove tastes from deep frying fat, fry potato slices in fat until brown. Removes taste so you can use fat again.

13. To get maximum amount of juice from lemon, warm in water. Press down firmly and roll on hard surface before juicing.

14. Shake raisins or chopped dried fruit with some of the flour before adding to cake batter. It will keep them from sinking to bottom of cake.

15. Place unripe fruit in brown paper bag to speed ripening.

16. Place tomatoes in brown paper bag and pour boiling water over sack until bag breaks. Tomatoes will be ready to peel.

17. Save leftover vegetables in the freezer; when you've saved enough, use them in stews and soups.

18. Wrap fresh vegetables in damp paper towels and put in plastic bags before refrigerating. They'll last longer.

19. Chill meat or chicken before coating with flour. Coating sticks better. Or dip meat in slightly whipped egg white.

20. Use toasted dry bread chopped in a blender instead of flour to thicken casseroles.

21. Before opening a package of bacon, roll lengthwise back and forth into a tube shape with your hands. Slices loosen and separate easier when you open package.

22. For very thin slices of beef or chicken, slightly freeze the meat before cutting. Cut slices across grain.

23. Empty leftover cereal or cookie crumbs into blender. Grind and store in airtight container. Use instead of graham crackers for tasty pie crust or dessert topping.

24. Break eggs into measuring cup before measuring shortening. Empty cup, then measure shortening. It won't stick.

25. Buy onions during harvest season. Put in old pantyhose leg, tying a knot between each onion. Hang in cool, dark place. When you need an onion, simply release the onion by cutting above the bottom knot.

Index

Recipe Index

(by Category)

Recipe Index
(Alphabetical)

NESTING, *COCOONING*
BURROWING...

That is what America is doing in the '90s ...
and Dian Thomas shows how to make it easy and fun

Americans are finding their greatest pleasures at home. Enjoying their families. Entertaining their friends. And they're looking for ways to do it easily and inexpensively. Now you can get in on the excitement. Choose from Dian's complete assortment of books and videos.

Let the fun begin!

Holiday Fun

Dian Thomas is back, with a year's worth ... ma years' worth ... of fun for readers. In **Holiday** she treats you to exciting ideas that turn mere holiday observances into opportunities to exer your imagination and turn the festivity all the up!! **Holiday Fun** gives you a year-round coll of festive ideas and recipes to make every holi special. You'll discover interesting tidbits of inf tion about many holidays, why we observe the and how to celebrate them with fun. You'll dis ideas for:

- A super Super Bowl party
- Silly April Fool's Day pranks
- An exciting egg hunt for Easter
- Homemade gifts for Mother's Day and Fathe
- Labor Day recipes and ideas for a family get-together
- Eerie decorations, creative costumes, and spooky treats for Halloween
- Creative Christmas ideas ...

... and more. From New Year's to Christmas.

Holiday Fun is loaded with creative and fun tips, recipes, and decorations. Dian's ideas are winners!! 176 pages, full-color photos. **$19.99.**

ORDER TOLL FREE: 1-800-846-6355

FUN AT HOME WITH DIAN THOMAS

This collection of creative ideas, demonstrated on ABC's *Home* show, has something for everyone. Dian shows you how to keep the kids busy on a rainy day, make Kick-the-Can Ice Cream, and craft unique holiday decorations. It's a treasure of fun do-it-yourself or with-your-children projects! 200 pages with over 500 illustrations. **$14.95.**

Backyard Roughing It Easy is synonymous with fun! In this book, Dian takes you on an outdoor adventure with her creative ideas for family fun. Dian answers all of your questions from how to start a fire to the do's and don'ts of planning a backyard camping trip with your family. Don't have a grill? Why not turn an ash can into a newspaper stove? Need tips for easy outdoor entertaining? Look no further; Dian's recipes and party ideas will make you the talk of the town. *Backyard Roughing It Easy* is filled to the brim with innovative, yet practical tips for outdoor living. You'll never look at your backyard the same again.

ROUGHING IT EASY

Even the camp cooks have fun when they're **Roughing It Easy!** This *New York Times* best-seller is chock-full of recipes and great ideas that make outdoor camping and cooking an adventure. It is the complete camper's bible. Cook eggs and bacon in a paper bag, boil water in a paper cup, and start a fire with steel wool and batteries! There are suggestions for equipment selection, fire building, campfire cooking, and even drying your own foods for backpacking! If you love the out-of-doors, **Roughing It Easy** is for you. 240 pages. **$14.99.**

DUTCH OVEN COOKING BASICS

TV personality Dian Thomas, an avid Dutch oven cook, is your guide to learning everything you need to know about getting started with Dutch oven cooking. She walks you step-by-step through the process as she energetically prepares delicious recipes and shows unique ways to use your oven.

Filmed in Utah, the heart of Dutch oven country, this video gets down to the very basics of Dutch oven cooking. Helpful tips take the viewer through oven selection, seasoning, cleaning, and storing. 30 minutes. **$9.95.**

VIDEOS

• **Let's Party!** • **Quick & Easy Holiday Ideas** • **Creating Fun & Easy Toy Projects**

Each video gives you step-by-step instructions and patterns for unforgettable party ideas, holiday decorations, and fun toys! 30 minutes. **$9.95** each.

DER BY MAIL OR CALL TOLL FREE 1-800-846-6355

Send with payment or credit card information to:
The Dian Thomas Company, PO Box 171107, Holladay, UT 84117
or **call TOLL FREE 1-800-846-6355.**

Name _____

Address _____

City/State/ZIP_____

Telephone (   ) _____

☐   Check/Money Order (please, no currency)
     Make checks payable to: **The Dian Thomas Co.**

☐ Visa   ☐ MasterCard   ☐ Discover   ☐ American Express

Signature_____ Exp. Date_____

Card Number_____
                  (Please list all numbers on card)

DESCRIPTION	QTY	UNIT PRICE	TOTAL
Holiday Fun		19.99	
Roughing It Easy		14.99	
Fun at Home		14.95	
Backyard Roughing It Easy		14.99	
Dutch Oven Cooking Basics video		9.95	
Let's Party! video		9.95	
Quick & Easy Holiday Ideas video		9.95	
Creating Fun & Easy Toy Projects video		9.95	

*Add $3.00 shipping/handling for first item and
$1.00 for each additional item.

Subtotal $_____

Shipping and handling* $_____

Utah residents add 6.25% sales tax $_____

• Canadian residents add 30% to total.

TOTAL $_____

Notes and Ideas